Not My Kid

Not My Kid

A Family's Guide to Kids and Drugs

by
Beth Polson
and
Dr. Miller Newton

ARBOR HOUSE
New York

*To our famlies for all their love and support
and to all the parents and kids whom we interviewed
for their inspiration.*

Copyright © 1984 by Beth Polson and Miller Newton

*All rights reserved, including the right of reproduction
in whole or in part in any form. Published in the United
States of America by Arbor House Publishing Company and
in Canada by Fitzhenry & Whiteside, Ltd.*

Library of Congress Cataloging in Publication Data

Polson, Beth.
  Not my kid.

  Bibliography: p.
  Includes index.
  1. Children—Drug use.   2. Drug abuse—Prevention.
I. Newton, Miller.   II. Title.
HV5824.C45P64   1984   362.2'93'088054   84–11069
ISBN 0–87795–633–2

Manufactured in the United States of America

10 9 8 7 6 5 4 3 2 1

Contents

Acknowledgments

To Bill W., Dr. Bob and all the old-timers of Alcoholics Anonymous for discovering the laws of the disease and the spiritual path of recovery. And to E. M. Jelnick and Vernon Johnson for their pioneering work in the progressive stages of the disease.

To Marilyn Pavkovic for her dedication and support and for her patience in typing this manuscript.

To Linda Evans, Judy Kickliter and Judy Rubino for assisting with typing at odd times and odd places.

To all the staff professionals and peer counselors for their help with the glossary and for their information and wisdom about kids getting in trouble with drugs and families getting well.

And to Frank Cooper for shepherding an idea into a reality.

Introduction
by Dr. Miller Newton

One night in March of 1979, Mark, barely fifteen, came home stumbling drunk. Our family was shocked. Ironically, at the time I was serving as the executive director of the state association of alcohol treatment programs in Florida, and my wife, Ruth Ann, was a supervising counselor at the publicly funded alcohol treatment agency in Tampa, Florida. Mark was the youngest of our three children. His older brother, Miller, was nineteen, and his sister, Johanna, was twenty. They were both healthy, normal and achieving young people.

The family banded together to deal with the crisis of what we assumed was Mark's first experiment with alcohol. The following morning we attempted, without moral judgment or rancor, to give Mark information about alcoholism in our family tree and about the dangers of mood-altering substances for an adolescent. As a family, we began to monitor his behavior closely. We perceived ourselves to be a healthy family with a

1

balance between strict supervision with relevant consequences and care and involvement in the activities of the children.

Mark was an interesting kid who exhibited unusual physical coordination and who had a very bright and inquiring mind. He had developed strong interests in marine biology, scuba diving (he was certified as a diver at age eleven) and wind surfing. He had a strong interest in his own health, frequently criticizing his older siblings for their "junk food" habits. He seemed to be "safe," considering his obsession with exercise and clean living. The first drunk episode was a cold dash of reality for the family. As we closely monitored his comings and goings, his activities, his appearance, his friendships and his schoolwork, conflicts within the family increased. Our anxiety about and fear for him intensified.

Two months later, the second drunk episode erupted in an outburst of physical violence—in a family that had *never* been very physical or very violent. Mark lost control with his brother and subsequently made killing threats toward both his brother and me. This resulted in a family conference in my study the following day with profuse tears, admission of having "tried pot" and a family "bottom line" of treatment for Mark, should he continue use of alcohol or pot. The months that followed were ones of close family supervision. Our small subdivision included 140 homes in a rural area. It was easy to check on Mark's whereabouts. On weeknights he had to be in at 9:00 P.M. and on weekend nights 11:00 P.M. The four of us—Ruth Ann, the other two children and I—made at least four tours of the neighborhood to check on his whereabouts each night.

Four months elapsed. Tension grew. As did Mark's hair. Family communication deteriorated. On Sunday night, September 23, the night of Miller's twentieth birthday, Mark had not been where he was supposed to be on one of the routine surveys during the evening. We found him with a group of guys riding around the neighborhood and called him home immediately for dishonesty. Slammed door, moody silence, loud rock music behind the door, as his brother, his mother and I discussed the issue. Mark went to sleep. When Miller entered the room at 12:30 A.M., he noticed a gleam of light reflected off a metal object on Mark's desk. That light turned out to be a pot pipe. We shook down the room and discovered paraphernalia, several stashes of pot and evidence of other drugs. The worst was true. We had been living in a fantasy about our ability to control his behavior. When Mark admitted trying pot, he was already smoking pot four to five days a week. By now he had graduated from regular pot and beer use to occasional pill use, speed and downs. And Ruth Ann and I were in the chemical abuse treatment field. It was right under our noses and yet, like so many parents, we hadn't seen a thing. Three days later, faithful to our promises of bottom lines, Mark entered an adolescent rehabilitation program in St. Petersburg.

Ruth Ann and I first came to the program on the Monday night after Mark's "bust." Heartbroken, more than a little scared, the tears rolled down our faces as we listened to other children talk about their drug use and their behavior—much like Mark's. We also heard parents sharing their feelings with their children, and the children talking about changes they were making in their lives. It was evident that the treatment program's building was a place where miracles happen. A place that gives kids a chance to come back from the behavior and feelings that go with drug use. And it helps families learn to laugh again.

Mark entered the program on September 26, 1979. Four months later I joined the staff. In the months that have followed, I have personally dealt with 3,000 young people and their families who have been involved with drugs. Mark is now twenty years old. He has been drug free for almost four years, works full time, goes to college and has the aspirations and lifestyle of a normal, healthy young adult.

But while Mark worked on his own recovery, I began to learn some things too. First, I learned about how kids get into drugs through peer influence. And then how they move in an orderly way through stages of worsening use, deteriorating behavior and diseased feelings. I learned how my own needs as a parent

made me deny my son's increasing involvement with drugs—
I didn't want my adequacy as a parent to be questioned. As a
matter of fact, my denial helped my son cover his increasing
use and deteriorating lifestyle. I also tuned in to a variety of
behaviors on my part that *helped* Mark with his drug use,
behaviors I learned to call "enabling." I also learned about my
own ambiguity as an adult, my ambivalence about my role as
a father—whether to be a pal to my son or a parent and authority figure. As my role changed from parent to staff member, I
began to work with other families, understanding their children's disease process, dealing with their own denial and enabling, and finally rebuilding their sense of self-worth as parents. Our common experience as parents of children with a
drug problem brought us to the door of treatment. The treatment itself helped us find the way back to reality, to health and
to wholeness.

Mark's death-to-life miracle at the treatment program and
the subsequent recovery of our entire family is the basis for this
book. Because of Mark's return to health, Ruth Ann and I joined
the staff of the program as an act of commitment and gratitude.
Later, at the invitation of another grateful parent whose child
we had helped, we left Florida to open a treatment center, KIDS
of Bergen County, Inc., in the New York metropolitan area. We
are expressing our continued gratitude, paying our debts for
Mark by bringing this treatment process to new families in a
new area of the country.

This book is a wider attempt to share what we learned in the
process of dealing with our own child's drug use and recovery
and in the process of working with many other families in
trouble. It is my hope that what I share in these pages will save
other families from the gut-tearing, heartrending, frightening
trial of adolescent drug use, and for others whose child is
already involved, it will help them with the awareness necessary to take a stand, to find treatment and to turn their tears
into laughter—as we did.

Introduction
by Beth Polson

Drug use is all-American, nondiscriminating and bipartisan. It sneaks into your home and tears your family apart. Because you are unsuspecting, it goes out of control before you can do anything about it.

Your daughter is pretty and popular. She's the homecoming queen and the editor of the school paper. So you think you're safe. You're not.

Your son is on the swimming team, a star athlete. He's talking about going to medical school. So you think you're safe. You're not.

That's what brings me here: I'm just like you. I thought you were safe too. What a kid needs today is self-esteem, right? Something to make him feel good about himself. A stable home life. And you'll get by. Wrong.

I'm a journalist. I live in an urban area. I work in the entertainment industry. And I thought kids on drugs were problem

5

kids. I thought they came from divorced or uncaring parents or, at the very least, both parents working. I thought druggie kids had long hair and looked "spaced out."

Then I produced a documentary called "Getting Straight" for NBC News. And I found out just how wrong I was. I found out it's what we don't know that's killing our children.

Kids today are not just "trying" marijuana. They're getting high on everything from Raid to tea bags, and they're doing everything from stealing money out of mom's purse to turning to prostitution to buy drugs.

Mind you, these aren't just high school and college kids. Drugs are on junior high school and elementary school campuses all over this country.

A twelve-year-old boy with freckles who looks as if he belongs in a cornflake commercial says he bought and sold acid at school.

A pretty little girl with pigtails and braces tells how she sneaks out her bedroom window at night to meet her friends and get high.

Another little girl—only twelve—says she's been using drugs since she was six.

A fifteen-year-old boy goes to meet his friend to get high. Not grass or coke or LSD. They're bored and they want to experiment. They break into a funeral home and steal embalming fluid. Bet you didn't know parsley dipped in embalming fluid gets you high, did you?

A high school freshman buys drugs at school—not from another student but from a teacher.

A teenage girl baby-sits for children in the neighborhood. She gets her charges high.

A graduating senior from Cincinnati, Ohio, says he only knows of two kids in his class who haven't tried drugs.

Drugs in America.

Not a ghetto problem. Not a suburban problem. Not a problem of divorced parents. Not a working parent's problem. Drugs are everywhere and they're everybody's problem. They're in big cities and in small rural communities. They strike troubled families and families whose children are seeming achievers, good students, athletes, prom queens.

And if you don't have children of your own and you think it's not your problem, you're wrong. There's a burglary being committed every eight seconds in this country, and a good number of them are being committed by kids on drugs. Kids start out stealing from their own parents. First, they take money from mom's purse. Then things start to disappear from the house—a camera, a clock-radio, anything they can sell. Quick money, easy high. Then shoplifting from the convenience store, a department store or the local grocery store. Next it's a neighbor's house. Then a stranger's—your house or mine.

The government has tried to stop the flow of drugs into this country. It isn't working. Drugs are available. Readily available. And there are an estimated four million people between the ages of twelve and seventeen taking drugs on a regular basis. And another three and a half million with an alcohol problem. But is there something that the family can do to help children deal with the peer pressure to use drugs, the constant exposure and temptation and society's message to "feel good"?

That is the purpose of this book: to give you, as parents, a better understanding of the drug problem that may exist in your own home, help you cope with it and give your family a chance to work again; to share with you what I learned doing the documentary and what I have learned in the two years that I have been researching this book. I have interviewed more then three hundred kids and families (many of their names have been changed in the chapters that follow). They come from different parts of the country and different socioeconomic backgrounds, but the horrifying tangled webb of a family in trouble with drugs is an all-too-familiar profile.

This is a book about family storms—how to predict them, how to weather them when they hit and how to find some blue skies.

It's a book about being a parent in difficult times, something nobody is automatically equipped to do. You need a permit or a license to drive a car, fly a plane, own a dog, import a rug, build a house, comb a coif, turn on a radio transmitter, sell a hot dog or shoot a duck—but you don't need any kind of permit to have a baby.

The fact is that being a parent is a big, expensive responsibility and an emotional task for which most people are ill prepared. Suddenly one day you've got your arms and heart full of this beautiful, bald, wet little bundle of big eyes and big lungs, and you realize you don't have any idea how to turn it into a person. There's no instruction manual. You're on your own.

You work hard at learning how to be a good parent. You go to all the PTA meetings, plan family outings, make sure everybody gets their dental checkups.

You get through the measles and the mumps by calling the doctor, asking friends what they did and reading a few books on child care and home medicine. But drugs are different. A kid on drugs doesn't break out in raspberry-colored splotches. You can't take his temperature to monitor his progress and you can't call a doctor to fix it.

But perhaps through the experience of other families, there is something to be learned.

What Dr. Newton and I offer you is observation and advice that has grown out of experience and other people's pain. What we hope it gives you is a chance for a drug-free, healthy family life.

1

Parent Denial
"Not my kid, couldn't happen to my kid."

Are you one of those parents who's lucky enough not to have to worry about your family being threatened by drugs? Are you thankful every day that there aren't drugs in your school, your neighborhood or your home? Or, more realistically, do you know that drugs are in your school, maybe even your neighborhood, but that at least your child would never get involved?

Are you truly part of that rare percentage of the parents of adolescents in this country whose children have never tried drugs? Or are you just practicing Parent Denial?

Think about it. Do you ignore the fact that your child sits listlessly through dinner, not getting involved in family conversation? Is the loud music coming from his room about to drive you to distraction but you don't dare say anything to him for fear it will spark a family argument? Does it worry you that your child reads so much that he uses eye drops all the time just to clear his eyes?

If you answered yes to any of these questions, Parent Denial may already be threatening the safety of your child—and only you can stop it. Parent Denial is an adult drug. Every parent takes it in one form or another—and some parents take lethal doses of it, just to ward off bad feelings. Any parent high on the denial drug is an accomplice to the conspiracy that leads a child to a druggie lifestyle. Other parents have learned the hard way.

Eric was only fourteen when he started coming home from school every day with red eyes. When his mother asked him about it, he blamed it on too much chlorine in the school pool. She believed him.

Cathy was a good student, always made As and Bs. When her report card showed a sudden drop in grades, and her mother wanted to know why, Cathy answered, "My teachers are terrible this year. All the good teachers are at the private schools." Mom marched off to school and gave the principal a piece of her mind.

John was arrested for selling drugs. He was only seventeen. He told his parents that yes, he was with some kids who had drugs but that the other kids were using them, not him. He didn't have anything to do with it. His father spent $25,000 in legal fees trying to prove his son was innocent.

When Carol came in late one night and stumbled into the bathroom, her mother went running after her. Carol spent the next three hours throwing up. Her mother thought she had the flu. When the incident happened a second time, her mother started to worry. Carol said she thought some kids had put some drugs in her soft drink. Her mother was furious. She wondered what kids—other people's kids—were coming to.

Donna was out of the house when her mother discovered marijuana in her room. As soon as Donna walked in, her mother confronted her. Donna kept her cool. "Oh, that, it belongs to Suzy. She asked me to keep it for her." Her mother reluctantly accepted the explanation but just to be on the safe side decided to have an "open" discussion about drugs with Donna.

"Have you ever tried drugs?" her mother asked. "Yeah, once," Donna answered, nonchalantly. Her mother, stunned by the fact that her little angel would even touch drugs, was nonetheless relieved that at least she had only tried it once.

Clearly her mother was playing in her court and Donna knew she had the ball—so she decided to run with it. "Yeah, I tried it," she said. "Just because all the other kids were trying it. But I didn't see what the big deal was about. It tasted awful. I hated it." Mom was getting more relief by the minute. And Donna knew it.

"I don't know why kids do it. I really don't. I mean, Mom, you don't know. A lot, I mean a lot of kids use drugs. I wish Suzy didn't do it. I've tried to talk to her about it but she won't listen. She's really a nice girl too, Mom, and I've told her she doesn't need drugs. But she keeps right on doing it. It's too bad. But I can tell you one thing, you don't have to worry about me."

Her mother walked out of the room, almost glowing. Wasn't it nice that she and her teenage daughter had such an honest, open relationship? Why is it that some parents have such a hard time talking to their teenage kids?

These situations represent five classic cases of Parent Denial. Five cases of parents who, when given blatant proof of a child's drug use, believed any possible excuse to avoid the reality—a kid, their kid, on drugs.

Parent Denial. What is it? Where does it come from? What does it mean? Who does it?

Denial does for your emotions what shock does for your body: It protects you from the pain. When the body is traumatized, your system secretes depressants to kill the pain. The blood flow slows down to protect the body from loss of blood, depriving the brain of sufficient oxygen and sending the body into physiological shock.

By the same token, denial lets parents put on blinders, protecting their minds and their emotions from pain. But in the case of kids in trouble with drugs, the protection doesn't help anyone: Parent Denial is dangerous.

The dictionary says denial is "refusal to admit the truth

. . . refusal to accept or acknowledge reality." Parent Denial is the world's best drug defense mechanism. It (a) keeps you from having to face the problem, (b) keeps the family name intact and (c) allows you to go on being the "world's best parent."

The bad news is that for every time you deny the reality of a child's drug use, you give him one less chance at a clean, healthy, drug-free life.

Are you guilty of Parent Denial? Do you always believe the best about your child? Do you ignore warning signals?

Have any of these things taken place in your home? Has your child called you a "no-good son of a bitch"? Has any one of your kids punched a hole in the wall in a fit of rage or frustration? Are there a lot of arguments in your house? Does your child's room look weird—lots of posters, beer bottles, strange pipes and things you don't understand? Does your child bring home a lot of "crazy-looking" kids? Does your child spend a lot of time in the bedroom, away from the rest of the family? Do you hear loud rock music coming from your child's room? Does your child sleep a lot? Do curfews get ignored? Are grades slipping at school? What about last year's passionate interest (scuba diving, horseback riding, cheerleading, track), is it passé this year? Does your child have his own supply of eye drops to "take the red out"?

If you answered "yes" or even "sometimes" to any of the questions, you may be missing the warning signs for early-to-middle drug use. And if you've been ignoring these signs, you too are guilty of Parent Denial.

Perhaps you've attributed these signs to growing up. You know, "Kids aren't like they used to be." You probably thought these things were just the usual potholes and ruts in the road of adolescence. Well, think again. That's just one of the many kinds of Parent Denial.

You see, Parent Denial takes several forms. Let's examine the different types of denial and why parents buy stock in them.

MINIMIZING BEHAVIOR

"THAT WASN'T SO BAD, NOW WAS IT?"

Frank was on the way home from the office one day, not looking forward to being hit with the latest in the series of "you know what your son did today" problems by his wife, Rosemary. He was tired of hearing it. Why couldn't she work it out? After all, she's the one who's home all day. He had to go out there and slay the dragons of the business world. Worse yet, she had started to call him at the office to complain about Kenny, his problems at school, how abusive he had become with her. And boy, did Frank hate that. Not only did he not have time to deal with it but suppose his secretary or some of his coworkers or, worse yet, his boss, were to get wind of the fact that his son was playing around with drugs. That would look real bad.

The closer he got to the house, the bigger the knot in his stomach grew. Then, just as he rounded the corner to the house, he spotted Kenny and some of his druggie friends in the front yard. He felt himself getting mad. He had warned Kenny to keep those kids away from there. He didn't want them on his property. They looked bad and it was their fault that Kenny kept getting into trouble.

He told himself to stay calm, it wouldn't do anybody any good for him to lose control. He pulled into the driveway but even before he could get the car door open, he spotted the beer cans. Drinking beer and smoking pot, that's all these kids did. But the nerve! Right there in his own driveway. Before he knew it, he was yelling at Kenny and ordering the other kids to get the hell off his property. Kenny started defending his friends. Then he pushed his dad.

Frank says he doesn't know what happened next. He just remembers throwing Kenny across the hood of the Oldsmobile and then Rosemary running out of the house in tears, trying to stop him.

This story isn't all that unusual for a family out of control, fighting the drug war. What is unusual about it is how this incident turned into one of Parent Denial.

A few weeks went by and Frank was at the ninth tee, his usual Wednesday afternoon golf game with the guys. The fellas were all talking about their sons, how fast they'd grown up, becoming the men they were. Some of them were bragging about their sons' athletic prowess when Frank chimed in.

"Yeah," he said, "I can't believe how strong my son Kenny is. You know, we were out in the driveway the other day, just playing around, and he almost whipped me. I mean he could have if he'd really wanted to. Yeah, that boy of mine is going to be a big man."

What *was* Frank talking about? Did he mean the same incident? He sure did. What he was doing was minimizing his son's behavior, partly to himself, but certainly to his golf buddies. What he told the guys may not have been important, but what he was telling himself was. Frank was engaged in Class A, topflight Parent Denial.

There are many ways parents choose to minimize their child's behavior, both to themselves and to others. When a grandparent expresses concern about the appearance of one of his grandchildren, a parent is likely to come to the rescue with comments like, "Oh, things are different today. That's the way all kids dress." To themselves, parents minimize behavior with things like, "Well, he may not dress well, but at least my child isn't _____." You can fill in the blank for yourself, anything will do so long as it perpetuates the false sense that everything with your children is okay. If their grades drop radically, at least they're going to school, not running all over the neighborhood during the day like the Jones' kids down the street. If they are a discipline problem, at least they've never run away from home. If they hang out in the malls or video arcades with "weirdo-looking" kids, better that than drugs. Well, listen up: All these are signs of early drug use and denial only draws the roadmap to middle and *advanced* drug use.

ACCEPTING THE CON

"DID YOU HAVE A NICE TIME AT THE PARTY, DEAR?"

There are some standard cons in the adolescent drug world: the chlorine in the pool excuse for red eyes, the keeping-drugs-for-a-friend and plenty of others, ranging from the car breaking down to the most elaborately woven tales imaginable. Most parents don't want to believe they are gullible enough, stupid enough, to get conned. After all, parents are worldly, wise, mature, experienced—surely they can see through the loose imagination of a teenager, right?

Consider this case: Maureen had gotten her three sons through the teenage years without much trouble. Oh, there was the broken leg from football and a couple of reckless driving tickets but nothing too serious. But somehow having a daughter was harder—or maybe she never should have had a baby at the age of forty anyway. Whatever it was, fourteen-year-old Elaine was giving her a run for her money.

First, Maureen told Elaine she could not go out on school nights. But then Elaine started leaving the house through the bedroom window. Instead of putting her foot down, Maureen changed the rules. Elaine could go out on school nights but she had to be home by ten o'clock. That didn't work either. Elaine never made it home on time and ignored all the restrictions her mother tried to impose as punishment. And weekends? Well, Maureen was relieved if she heard the front door shut by two in the morning. The constant conflict made Maureen more than a little battleweary.

So, when the night came that Elaine didn't come home at all, Maureen sat silently in the living room, sobbing, praying that her daughter, the little girl she had wanted so much and waited for so long, was safe.

Finally, just about daybreak, Elaine slowly sneaked open the front door. She was surprised to find her mother sitting there in her housecoat. "Mom," she said, "what are you doing up?" Then, never missing a beat, she launched into a convoluted story about where she had been.

"Mom, the worst thing happened, you're never going to believe it. You know my friend Judy. The pretty one with the long blonde hair. Well, she's been going out with this guy named Gary for a long time. Well, tonight, she came out to the roller skating rink and she told me that she thought Gary was going out with some other girl. She was crying and she was so upset. So we borrowed a friend's car and went to look for him. Then, we saw a friend of his who said that Gary had driven down to the beach for the weekend so we went to look for him. We drove all the way down there and then we couldn't find him. But we were so tired we knew it wouldn't be safe to drive all the way home so we thought it would be better to sleep for a couple hours. So that's what we did. Then about four o'clock we drove home. It was an easy drive coming back because there was nobody on the road. I started to call you. I knew you'd be worried. But we were never near a phone. And I knew you wouldn't want me driving when I was tired. So I did what I thought was best. I sure felt sorry for Judy though. What a clod that guy Gary is. Oh well, Mom, I'm going to bed. I need some sleep. You'd better go to bed too. You shouldn't stay up and worry about me. You know I'll be all right."

Elaine wandered off to her room. And Maureen whispered a little prayer, thanking God that her daughter was safe.

Well, her daughter wasn't safe. Her daughter had spent the entire night getting high with her friends and Maureen was the victim of a teenage drug con.

One of the biggest drug cons going is the art of throwing the attention on someone else. Chris: "I would tell my mom that I thought my brother Eric was doing drugs with his friends just so she'd think I was really straight."

Playing the good kid is the best way of keeping parents in the dark—and kids know it. John: "I knew it wasn't worth blowing. I needed them to support me. I needed my allowance to buy drugs. I couldn't risk it. They had to think I had my act together and wouldn't go near drugs."

It is not unusual to find that a son can con his mother and a daughter can con her father. Renee: "I manipulated my dad a lot. I would go to my mom and ask her something. If she said no I would go to my dad and ask him. He was always scared to say no because he was scared of what I would do. So then I'd go back and tell my mom that Dad said it was okay." All parents have experienced this kind of con, whether their kids are doing drugs or not. But it is a particularly good con for druggies in their bid for more freedom—getting out of the house.

Another standard among druggie and nondruggie kids is the "all the other kids' parents let them do it, why can't I?" con. This one works wonders because it leaves the burden of proof on the parent. Most parents are not going to call up other parents and question what their rules and regulations are—it might make them look silly, not in control. It's usually guilt that forces them into submission. No parent wants to be THE square parent in the neighborhood. This con may not work all the time but odds are it will pay off for the druggie kid a good percentage of the time.

The art of conning used by kids on drugs is really no different than that used by the used car salesman or the aluminum siding man. The only difference is it's not your car or the paint on your house that's at stake. It's your child's choice to do drugs—and his emotional and physical health.

IGNORING ADVICE

"IT'S NONE OF YOUR BUSINESS."

Often parents get the warning flag from schoolteachers, a principal, a police officer, a neighbor or even another family member. But any good denier worth his salt can ignore those people. They're outsiders. "What do they know about raising my kid?"

The Hoags were a nice family. They went to church every Sunday, went camping together on weekends. The parents had a good marriage. In fact, they were involved in teaching marriage workshops. You know, how to keep your family together, how to keep the spark in your marriage and how to keep your kids on the straight and narrow.

Well, one weekend they were away teaching just such a workshop. They left their two teenagers—an older daughter and a younger son—at home.

Their son recalled how it went. "It was great. I used to look forward to those weekends because I knew they'd be gone Friday night, all of Saturday and wouldn't be back until sometime late Sunday." That meant easy street. A whole weekend with nobody to ask where you'd been, who you'd been with or what you'd been doing—a license to do as many drugs as possible in a three-day period.

But, you say, there was no way the parents could know, no reason why they shouldn't leave those kids alone. Hold on a minute. That's not exactly true. In fact, they had had plenty of signs.

First, there was the trouble with their son at school. Teachers suspected drug use. But Mom knew better. You see, her son was small for his age, had some health problems and those teachers just didn't understand him. Warning number one.

Then there was the money that disappeared. Already, we know the Hoags are a good churchgoing family. Well, Mom is on the committee that collects money to be given to less fortunate families. Only the money started to disappear. A family member suggested half-jokingly that maybe one of the kids "borrowed" from the fund. Mrs. Hoag's reaction? "How dare you say such a thing." Warning number two.

Several times the neighbors had casually wondered aloud what the kids did all those weekends that the parents were away. But the parents weren't worried. Their kids were responsible, no problem leaving them alone. A couple of times the neighbors had gone so far as to suggest there seemed like an awful lot of kids going in and out of the house when the parents were gone. The parents wrote that one off as their children being popular, they'd always had a lot of friends. Warning number three.

Because of Parent Denial, the Hoags have ignored the warnings of teachers, family members and neighbors. But because they are into denial, they walk away for the weekend, leaving their kids free for a three-day high, while they go off to teach other people how to find the good life with their families.

THE BLAME GAME

"I HOPE YOU'RE HAPPY NOW. LOOK WHAT YOU'VE DONE TO YOUR KID."

Ah, yes. An old favorite. The Blame Game. As things start to go wrong, this is a good opportunity to take the blame off the kid's choice to do drugs (where it belongs) and lay it directly on the shoulders of your mate. This should tick one parent off just enough that he or she decides to square off with the other and slug it out verbally. "It's your fault because . . ." "No, it's your fault because . . ." Meanwhile, the kid's drug use continues.

A TYPICAL FATHER: "I blamed my wife for everything that was going on. I thought she was too strict on Lynn. I thought she wasn't giving her the freedom that she needed, she was a little too tight on her."

The Blame Game moves into the big leagues with single parents. The parent who's away (usually the father) blames the custodial parent for his or her inability to keep the kids under control. The at-home parent angrily blames the other for abandoning the family, not living up to his or her responsibilities.

Take the Burtons. Their nineteen-year-old son, Jim, started using drugs in the seventh grade. He used pot, hash, hash oil, opium, ups, downs, acid, Thai stick, mushrooms, PCP, THC, morphine, mescaline, cocaine and painkillers.

JIM: "I had no feelings left. I remember my friend got stabbed to death and I didn't even cry. I'd get in constant fights with my family and I didn't even care. It was like all my senses were tuned out. I was having to take five hits of acid just to get off.

"I'd come home at night and cry. I'd be tripping on acid and I'd come in and I'd be coming down and I'd go through a lot of depressed feelings. And I'd just sit there and cry. I remember one night I just went in and threw my guts up and then I just laid on the bed and wished I were dead, I felt so bad. I remember four or five different times, I'd go in my mom's room and I'd give her a hug and I'd cry and I'd promise her I'd never do acid again.

"I just thought everything was going wrong with my life. My parents were separated. I blamed my drug problem on that, mainly. It was my dad's fault. I hurt and I'm using drugs to feel better."

MRS. BURTON: "I thought, this poor kid, his father and I are separated and it's a time when a boy needs his father most. He of my three children is the most insecure. I can take care of the girls but he really needs his father."

Meanwhile, Mr. Burton blamed his wife for being weak and letting the situation get out of hand. Everybody blamed something other than the problem—Jim's decision to do drugs.

In fact, this may be a case of which came first, the chicken or the egg, the separation or the drugs. While everybody blamed the drugs on the separation, could it be that all the problems with Jim were the reason Mr. Burton started taking more and more trips out of town, then started taking longer and longer trips and eventually decided to move out? The Blame Game muddied the waters, so it's hard to tell. But one thing is certain: Hiding behind this form of Parent Denial allowed Jim's drug problem to continue.

LOOKING FOR ANOTHER CAUSE
"TELL ME IT'S ANYTHING BUT DRUGS."

Parents would rather believe almost anything about their child —"he's sick," "he has a learning disability" or even "he's mentally ill"—than accept the fact that he's on drugs. And they'll go to all kinds of mental, emotional and even financial lengths to convince themselves of this.

A military family can always say, "The moves caused it." A parent of a child with any kind of health problem, no matter how minute, can say: "It's his loss of hearing." "It's because he's hyperactive." "It's because he's small for his age."

Take JoAnn. Her grades started to drop. Then she got caught smoking at school. Then she was hauled in for possession. Her father hit the roof—but at no point did he accept the idea that his daughter might have a drug problem. Instead, he spent $17,000 on a battery of tests and a series of psychiatrists looking for anything, anybody that would tell him that his daughter had a learning disability. Seventeen thousand dollars! Because he would rather his daughter have a learning disability than a drug problem.

Sharon was a dental hygienist. She was smart. And she was concerned about health care. When her daughter started coming home vomiting, night after night, Sharon became concerned. It wasn't the flu, there were no other symptoms. There had always been difficult times with Tracey. She was a gifted child. Teachers had said that gifted children were hard to handle. They had advised Tracey's parents "to be firm, to be loving and to hang on." Sharon thought about that advice when she hit the vomiting spells. Was it stress? Nerves? Too much pressure at school to excel? In eighth grade, they had taken Tracey to a psychiatrist and had spent over a thousand dollars on treatments but Tracey was still difficult. Sharon didn't think drugs were the problem—once they had caught Tracey smoking pot with her cousin and Sharon had immediately bought books and videotapes about the harmful effects of drugs, and she and Tracey had talked about it. "I really thought I was Supermom," Sharon recalled. "I really believed in discipline and I thought everything was going okay. Then that summer I heard her induce vomiting. I had seen a program on bulimia [an eating disorder similar to anorexia nervosa] on Phil Donahue. So I went to the National Institute of Health and started looking at cases. I thought, 'Oh, my God, my daughter has the beginnings of anorexia.' I got a book and read it and I saw Tracey on every page. I asked her to read it and she saw her personality in it. I thought I had really figured out what was wrong. I took her to five different doctors. At Children's Hospital, the doctor said, 'Let's say it's adolescent rebellion.' He patted her on the back. He said she had bulimia and she really had to shape up. I had done so much research to find out what was wrong."

What *was* wrong was that Tracey had been doing drugs for three years, mostly alcohol. We should take a moment here to stress that alcohol, just like cocaine or marijuana, is a drug— a mood-altering chemical. Don't *ever* try to tell yourself that it's not.

Tracey's mother went to unbelievable lengths to avoid admitting it was drugs—and in the meantime, Tracey was getting high regularly and then throwing up. "I felt like I was throwing up feelings . . . like all the anger inside me was out and flushed down the toilet and I felt relieved after I did it." But the feelings weren't always good. "I remember one time I got really drunk. And I was scared. I didn't know if I could make it to the bathroom. So my boyfriend held my dress back and I forced myself to throw up on the stairs. I spent about four hours sitting in the car with a blanket wrapped around me. It was my junior prom night and I had vomited all over my dress."

Tracey's mother was into Parent Denial. And Tracey used her mother's denial to hide her drug use. Sharon: "I finally couldn't take it anymore. Tracey is so much smarter than I am. And that scared me. There weren't drugs around when I was a kid and I just couldn't stay on top of things. Finally, I went to the National Federation of Parents for Drug Free Youth and the counselor said to me, 'Lady, you've got a drug problem.' But I said, 'No, you don't understand, it's bulimia. My daughter wouldn't do drugs. I educated her about drugs. She's too intelligent to do drugs.' " The denial continued.

KIDS WILL BE KIDS

"WHEN I WAS YOUR AGE . . ."

Ken was one of those lucky kids. His father had a good job. His mother didn't work. In fact, she prided herself on being Supermom. "I was a Boy Scout leader. I was a room mother. I took my children to school and picked them up every day. And I always made sure I had at least ten minutes a day alone with each child, one-on-one time. I'd ask them if they had any problems, anything they wanted to talk about. I'd always have a snack for them after school and I'd sit and talk with them."

Ken was in private school, barely passing. At home he was rebellious, spent a lot of time in his room alone and was continuously in family fights. He smoked pot every day before going to school and used harder drugs three or four times a week.

His parents allowed him to get a motorcycle if he'd promise to straighten up his act. He didn't. Instead, he got nine traffic tickets and eventually lost his license. His mother explained it away with, "Boys will be boys." She told his father, "Try to remember what you were like at his age."

Well, in fact, Dad admitted, he was a fighter and he always liked to brag about it. "My whole family was like that, not just me. It's the kind of things where you say you're Irish so you have a bad temper. It's been that way all my life. I can remember my oldest brother taking a golf club to his car because it wouldn't start, so when Ken stuck his fist through the garage door, it was nothing."

It was nothing, all right. Nothing but Parent Denial. He's my kid so he's bound to have a rough streak. And Mom could write it off to "like-father-like-son." Meanwhile, Ken's drug problem continued, hidden behind a veil of "boys will be boys."

NOTHINGS'S WRONG

"I DIDN'T SEE ANYTHING. DID YOU SEE ANYTHING?"

This is the most prevalent form of Parent Denial—the outright denial of the existence of *any* problem. And this brand of denial is usually accompanied by a heavy dose of rationalization.

If a child gives up parent-bankrolled horseback riding after years of interest, and you explain it away with "oh, she's dropped horses because now she's interested in boys" you're rationalizing.

If things start to disappear from the house and you blame it on the guy who came to fix the water heater, you're rationalizing.

If you know your child is stealing liquor from the family cabinet and partially refilling the bottles with water and you ignore it, you're denying.

If you acknowledge the fact that he uses a little pot with "but at least he's not using hard drugs," you're denying.

If your daughter lettered in swimming last year and dropped it this year and you think the coach didn't know how to work with her, you're denying.

If the family silver seems to be dwindling and you think the cleaning lady took it or somebody dropped it in the garbage disposal, you're denying.

Got the idea? Parent Denial comes in many forms. It lives inside of every parent. And it is lethal. So why would a parent who wants nothing but the best for his child, a parent who wants his kid to have an easier time of it, a chance at a better life, allow Parent Denial to blind him to reality?

It's simple. No parent wants to admit to being a failure at parenting, and having a kid on drugs translates as "I didn't measure up. I let my kid down. If only I had been a better mother . . . a better father, maybe this wouldn't have happened."

And it couldn't happen to your kid anyway, not if you were a good parent, right? You were always so careful to remember their vitamins and make sure they had their dental checkups. You don't want to think you've failed them now, not at this crucial stage, when they're just about to become adults and go out on their own.

A TYPICAL FATHER: "I didn't want to recognize that it was a drug problem because that would look bad for me. If I have a druggie kid, then my neighbor who thinks he's Mr. Straight will look at me and think I'm a loser. I didn't want to admit that my kid was a druggie and his kids weren't . . . which is really funny now because I've since found out his kids are druggies, too. I had a high stake in avoiding the failure feeling. It would look bad for me at home and worse at work. My daughter wanted to con me, lie to me and I wanted to believe her. I just didn't want to admit that I could have a druggie kid."

A TYPICAL MOTHER: "I thought she was just going through adolescence, trying to break away from the family. I never really saw her come home high because I didn't know what high was. I really never thought it could be drugs. Not my Donna. My Donna's been raised in a Christian home . . . we always went to church together. We're not alcoholics. We're not divorced. We don't fight. We're good parents."

Parent Denial also has to do with high stakes in a marriage. "If my child is on drugs, I am, therefore, a bad mother. I've really let my spouse down. I must be a bad wife too."

The one thing all parents have to accept when faced with a family drug problem is that PARENTS DO NOT MAKE KIDS TAKE DRUGS. You did not bend their elbow to take that first drink. You did not hold their fingers for that first marijuana joint. No matter what problems exist in your family, the kid who makes the decision to try drugs does so of his own free will. He does it knowing right from wrong. He does it knowing it violates certain values in society. He does it fearing he might get caught. *He* does it. Not you. He did not do it because you were too strict on him. He did not do it because he wasn't as smart as one of his siblings. He did not do it because he was smaller or weaker or bigger or stronger. He probably did it because friends told him it felt good or because he was curious or because he wanted to be liked. You're not Robert Young from "Father Knows Best" or Fred MacMurray from "My Three Sons." You're a real, living parent with hopes and dreams for your children, dreams that sometimes get sidetracked by reality. But reality is what you have to deal with, as much as you may not like it, as much as you may prefer to look the other way, as much as you may try to deny it.

Denial is merely a way of buying time. "If I ignore this situation maybe it will go away." Wrongs will somehow miraculously right themselves if you shut your eyes real tight and deny. You're dreaming.

Refusal to accept reality means that you go along your merry way never having to admit your family is out of control. Everyone wants to think of himself as being in control—especially parents. That's the way the whole parent-child relationship is supposed to work, isn't it? An out-of-control parent means that the child is left to fend for himself—and again, the parent feels that he has failed.

Does this sound familiar? "I used to spend hours with her telling her stories, lecturing her. But it didn't work. I was getting so frustrated that I couldn't help her. I wanted to be a good parent, not a failure. I wanted her to be a happy kid, not a kid with a problem like this. It seemed like I was yelling and screaming at her a lot because she wouldn't listen to me, she would never come home on time. Then when I tried to talk to her, she'd make snippy remarks or just stand there with a shit-eating grin on her face. I remember a time right before Christmas . . . I got so mad at her I started pushing her. I didn't care if she fell over a table or split her head open or anything.

I was so upset, so mad at her for ruining our Christmas. I was frustrated because she wouldn't listen to me. And I was hurt. Finally, I grabbed a suitcase and threw it at her. I told her to pack and get out of the house. I didn't want to see her anymore. At that point, I really felt bad about myself. I felt guilty. I couldn't believe what I was doing, what I was saying. I was trying to throw my own daughter out of our home."

Denial keeps a parent from having to admit that his expectations aren't being met. The father who wants his son to become a professional football player. The mother who wants her daughter to be beautiful, popular. Vicarious pleasures. Things parents most likely wanted for themselves—but now that *their* time for those things has come and gone, they want them for their children. Admitting to a child's drug problem means admitting that your expectations are not being fulfilled.

You think you can mold that little baby into anything you want. "I loved that little girl so much. We used to go shopping together, we did everything together. We were close. She was my little good buddy. And I was going to mold her into a great big, wonderful, happy child. When she started to have problems, I made excuses for her. I said it was because I had to work . . . she's just growing up . . . she's a wonderful child underneath. But the problems started getting really bad. Almost overnight, her personality changed. It was like my little girl left for school one day and a different little girl—the wrong girl—a bad, nasty girl came home in her place. I couldn't talk to her anymore. I didn't even know who she was. My perfect child. My beautiful daughter was going down the drain. Then one day she came home with a tattoo and I just wanted to kill her. I really did. I wanted to rip that child apart, beat her, tear her hair out. I was afraid of myself. Suddenly, I went cold. I thought, 'My God. My baby. What have I molded? What have I made?' "

This mother ended up driving herself to the hospital in the rain late at night, pushing the emergency button and asking to be admitted. When they asked her why, she told them because she was going crazy. She was crying hysterically and they let her in. It was her roommate in the hospital who said to her, "You're not crazy. It sounds to me like you have a daughter on drugs." This mother had been denying her daughter's drug problems for so long that it got to the point where she would rather check herself into a mental ward than admit that her daughter was on drugs.

If owning up to denial comes hard for you, if you have too much ego involved to admit you have an ego involved, you are not alone.

There was the retired police officer who worked all his professional life with people on alcohol and drugs. But when it came to his own son, he never recognized a thing.

"I could tell you about alcohol and how people respond to it. I knew about heroin, pushers and that sort of thing but I didn't know anything about what kids are doing today. I just thought Mike was being a resistive teenager."

Or the military colonel who was put in charge of the army's drug program. At home, he had three kids, all on drugs, and he never saw a thing.

THE COLONEL: "Let's face it, I was in a position of responsibility, a commander. My family was looked upon differently. They are officer's kids. And the indicators were there. I just didn't see them. Nancy would come home and cast on me and my wife some tremendous challenges as parents, you know, 'you sons-of-bitches, you're not good parents. I don't give a shit whether you live or die.' I was the classic denier, there's no question about it. I knew it was happening. I was smart enough about this business because I saw it all day in my people, my soldiers, and I was seeing it in my own family but I was just denying the hell out of it because I didn't want it in my family. That's the bottom line. I was living with drugs and alcohol fourteen, sixteen hours a day. When I came home, I didn't want any part of it.

"I didn't have drugs in my barracks. I wouldn't allow it. But I let it run rampant in my own home and did nothing about it. I couldn't even see it."

And what about the federal intelligence officer who came home from work one day and found his daughter working with a little plastic bag and a rubber band on the kitchen counter? She was cutting cocaine. She told him she was doing a project for a science class, making a parachute. And he believed her.

And then there's Lindy's family. Lindy: "I got into drugs through my church. My youth group was on a church retreat in North Carolina. I was pretty much, you know, straight but I wanted to be part of the crowd. I wanted the other kids to like me. So they introduced me to pot . . . I did pot and alcohol for about a year, you know, at church, and every once in a while at school."

Church? How could that happen? Where were her parents?

LINDY'S MOTHER: "I was with her at the church youth group. I was the counselor for the senior Methodist Youth Fellowship, and she was in the junior MYF. Mom didn't see a thing."

LINDY: "One time right before church group, this druggie friend of mine asked me to go to the bathroom with her. She had a bag of pills. I don't know what they were. I just started taking them. I don't remember anything else about that night. I went home and I don't even remember if I took my clothes off before I went to bed."

And where was Dad while all this was going on? Dad: "I was the church choir director. We were there every time she was there."

Right under their noses at church. And school? Dad was the school music teacher. Lindy went to his class high. Lindy: "I would sit in the back of the room and play very casual. I thought, 'Well, if he doesn't know, then I'll get away with it.' And I kept doing it for a long time."

LINDY'S FATHER: "I really didn't want to face it. I didn't want to admit that my daughter was a druggie. I was still living in a dream world, I guess. I thought we were doing the right thing. We went to church. Lindy was in my choir at church and my class at school. We camped together. We did all those things. I just didn't want to face it."

Denial is not something parents can easily stop. Remember, parents *want* to believe their kids. "God forbid the grandparents should find out. What would my sister say? What will the neighbors think? And the people at the bridge club?' " Even when parents learn the hard way, that is, through experience, Parent Denial continues. The Holden family is a good example.

John was the youngest of the three Holden children. His sister Margie was an achiever, a tennis player. When she started using drugs, it tore the family apart. You would think the Holdens would have learned how to spot the early signs of drug use, wouldn't you? Well, they didn't. Instead, it became part of their denial.

DAD: "I was sure John wouldn't do drugs. He saw what it did to his sister. He saw how it destroyed all of her wonderful college opportunities, her tennis career, everything she had going for her. This boy grew up with this horrible thing, seeing the screaming, the rages. He would never do it. I felt safe and complacent."

MOM: "We had no idea John was using drugs. If we had, we would have done something about it. We had already had one child throw her life away because of drugs. We certainly wouldn't let it happen to another one but we didn't know it. Parents expect to see a long-haired kid before they think about drugs. Our son was a scholastic example. Every time I would say anything to him or question him, he gave me all this intellectual stuff. I never went to college. I'm not too well-educated. And he threw up a smoke screen until I didn't know where I was."

Margie's drug use had made an impression on John. "I had sworn to my father I would never do drugs," he recalls. "I was in sixth grade. And I was so against drugs that I would look through my sister's room and find a joint and give it to my parents. I hated drugs. I hated what they were doing to my family."

But all that hate disappeared when John got to high school and found most kids doing drugs. Early on, things weren't so bad—he kept up his grades, stayed on the honor roll. But then the grades started to slip. His parents thought he needed a better school and a chance to meet some new friends. So they sent him off to boarding school—not knowing that this was like writing John a free pass for getting high every day. He did, however, go home weekends.

JOHN: "I would get high on Friday and then go home on the bus. Then Saturday was the only day I had to stay straight. Sunday I would go back to school and get high again. I'd sell things I got for Christmas up at school. If my parents asked what happened to my headphones, I'd say somebody took them. And it wound up, I'd sell a two-hundred-dollar tennis racquet for ten dollars just to get what drugs I could because I was really desperate. I sold a two-hundred-fifty dollar watch for ten dollars one time just to get some pills."

What John couldn't sell of his own, he'd shoplift—tape recorders, earphones, cassettes. And he stole from his parents. On one of his weekend trips home, he took his grandfather's gold railroader's watch, one of his mother's treasures. When he got back to school, he traded it for a quarter pound of pot. And the Holdens' were still denying. Their scholarly son had let his grades go, started hanging out with some new, "strange-looking" friends, he'd had to be sent off to boarding school, all his possessions (and some of theirs) had started to disappear, and they thought nothing was wrong.

John was doing pot, alcohol, rush, uppers, downers, hash, prescriptions, PCP, cocaine, solvents and glue. Eventually—on the Holdens' wedding anniversary, in fact—he was expelled from the boarding school. He came home. No private school would touch him. So he enrolled in public school. He managed to graduate and get into junior college. But things got worse. He overdosed a couple of times. Finally, his parents caught him red-handed on the beach, high with a friend. At last, they were forced to stop denying. They placed John in a drug program.

John did well, moved rapidly until eventually he was allowed to return to junior college. At school, he got right back into the scholastic swing. And the Holdens breathed a sigh of relief. One of them would pick him up from school every day, proud as punch. They had lost their daughter but saved their son. Until . . .

DAD: "One night we went to the campus to pick him up at the usual eight-fifteen. I was always bursting with pride every time I saw this great straight kid come swinging around the corner, books under his arm, clean-cut looking kid. So I sat there waiting for him and waiting for that good feeling I got every time I saw him. But then he didn't come. I looked all over the place for him. We went frantically all over campus. I was sure an emergency of some sort had come up . . . or maybe he'd gotten another ride home . . . or maybe he'd been kidnapped."

Everything occurred to the Holdens except the truth: Their son had gone back to drugs. Five minutes after he decided to run, he was getting high. Ten days after he decided to run, the needle was back in his arm, pumping the drugs into his body.

It's tragically simple. The Holdens had every reason not to practice Parent Denial. They had fought the battle once before. But something inside them made them continue to deny John's use of drugs. Over and over and over again.

Parent Denial plays as big a role in perpetuating the problem of kids and drugs as the pusher on the street corner. Because the parent who is into denial cannot see the problem, much less helf find a solution. Sticking your head in the sand leaves a lot of you exposed.

Here is a Parent Denial checklist that might help you get your head out of the sand. If any of these strike a nerve, you could have a problem. If several of them seem frighteningly familiar, you probably do have a problem. And if you recognize most of them, you may need help.

Parent Denial Checklist

1. Does your child have red eyes most of the time? Does he have his own supply of eye drops?
2. Are you ignoring changes in your child's behavior? Changes in grades? Changes in personality?
3. Do you attribute unacceptable behavior to "growing up" or "just being a kid"?
4. Do you blame your spouse for your child's problems?
5. Do you listen to your spouse or outsiders when they suggest that your child may have a problem with drugs? Or do you just get mad at the accuser?
6. Are you feeling like a failure as a parent?
7. Do you buy your child's stories that the drugs or paraphernalia you found in his room belong to a friend?
8. If you are a working mother, do you blame yourself for your child's problems because you're not at home? If you're a working father, do you blame yourself because you work such long hours, have to be on the road a lot?
9. If you went into your child's room right now, would you find any sign of drugs? What would you do if you did?
10. Are you blaming divorce or the absence of one parent in the home for your child's behavior?
11. Are you feeling anxious about the problems your child is having adjusting to growing up?
12. Has your child admitted trying marijuana? Will he talk about it?
13. Does he admit to smoking "only" pot? Do you believe him?

2
Kid Denial
"Drugs aren't my problem."

Kid Denial, like Parent Denial, is a big emotional shutdown device. It allows a druggie kid to deny that drugs are having any harmful effect on his life.

All kids on drugs practice denial. "Yeah, I use drugs but I can handle it." That's their way of convincing themselves that they are in control of the drugs and drugs are not in control of them.

"I'm cool. I want to use drugs. I like the cool drug lifestyle." Denial.

"I can stop any time I want to." Denial.

"Look, you don't know what it's like. You don't know anything about whether it's good for me or bad for me. You've never been high. You don't know how it feels. You're all screwed up. You don't know what the good life is like." Denial.

Kid Denial allows a drug user to attribute everything that is wrong in his life to something other than drugs. It can be another person, a certain situation, even society itself—but it's never drugs. Drugs are what make things better. They help him feel good.

If a kid gets busted for possession of marijuana, he says the cop who takes the pot uses it to get high himself. The cop's no good.

If a teacher confronts a student about fouling up in school, not living up to his potential, the kid says that he wants to quit school anyway. He's only going because he has to. And all those kids who make good grades are "goody-goodies." They're not cool. School's no good.

If John, whose father and grandfather were both doctors, has always dreamed of being a doctor himself and suddenly thinks medical school is dumb, he blames it on the fact that all doctors are in it for the money. It's a mercenary profession. The system stinks.

It's always something or somebody else that's the problem. It's the cops, it's teachers, it's the system, it's parents, but it is never, ever drugs. It's not drugs that cause those awful, depressed, horrid feelings. It's not drugs that make you throw your guts up, cry yourself to sleep at night or think you're going crazy. Drugs are only responsible for the good feelings.

KAY: "I blamed my mom and dad. My dad's never said, 'I love you,' or put his arm around me or hugged me. I told Mom and Dad that I hated them. I had a lot of fights with them . . . I mean physical fights. I was screwing up at school, and I blamed the teachers for that. I thought they didn't like me . . . that they thought I was stupid because I didn't understand some course I was failing. They'd pick on me all the time. They didn't understand me. I didn't think my problem was drugs because I wasn't showing any signs of being a big, bad druggie.

"Then I got pregnant and I even blamed that on my folks. If they'd given me more love, I wouldn't have been sleeping with this guy. I'd come home at night and sit in my room on the floor. I had posters all over my room. I'd turn the lights out and there would just be a little light from the streetlight coming in the window. And I'd sit there and I'd tell myself, 'You're going crazy, Kay, you're really going crazy. You're so sick. Your mom hates you. Your dad hates you, everybody hates you. You're ugly.' I never thought it could be drugs. Then I started to think about suicide. . . ."

DAVID: "I blamed it on everybody. When counselors asked me what was wrong with me, I would tell them my brother Michael was worse off than I was just to take the attention off of me. I would do it to manipulate them. Plus, if I really started to get in trouble, I always blamed it on the fact that I was different 'cause I just have one kidney. Then I knew that would make everybody feel sorry for me."

CARL: "I blamed my folks for my use of drugs. They would make me come home at nine-thirty on school nights and eleven-thirty on weekends unless I was going someplace special. So I told them I went to a lot of late movies so I could stay out 'til one in the morning. But I never went to movies. My friends could stay out all night long if they wanted to and their folks didn't do anything about that. I really resented it. I was really bitter. I thought they were on my back all the time and I hated to have to tell my friends that I had to go home when they were going to stay out for hours.

"I remember one time I even threw a party out at the beach, and I spent a hundred dollars, money I'd saved from my job, for drugs. I was getting everybody high and everybody felt good about me because I bought the drugs. And I had to be home at eleven o'clock. It was my party and I had to go home. All my friends stayed out there 'til three o'clock in the morning, getting high on my drugs, and I had to go home. That really made me mad. And I couldn't even take some of the harder drugs because I knew I had to go home and yet I was giving it away to other people. I just felt like my folks were too hard on me."

DENIAL TO OTHERS
"ME? DRUGS? NEVER."

Every kid knows that responsible adults—parents, teachers, coaches, relatives and neighbors—think that doing drugs is wrong. And because he wants to be considered straight by these people, it's important for him to deny any association with drugs. In the beginning, that's not so tough. He gets high every now and then with his friends, but he hangs onto those things that win him approval from adults. He still has a good relationship with his parents. His grades haven't started to slip yet. He still shows up for practice and can even perform well at the big game. His grandparents are proud of him. And he's really polite to all the neighbors. Remember Eddie Haskell in "Leave It to Beaver"? "Hello, Mr. and Mrs. Cleaver. My, Mrs. Cleaver, don't you look lovely today! Is Wallace at home? Of course, if he's doing his homework, I wouldn't want to disturb him."

Everybody still thinks he's on the straight and narrow. So much the better. The better to become a big, bad druggie, my dear. Because as long as nobody's the wiser, the heat is off and the freedom to continue using more and harder drugs will lead the kid straight down the road to disaster.

So far, all of this denial is conscious, well thought out, and well executed because drugs really haven't started to play that large a part in the kid's life. But with more drugs comes more denying and pretty soon the druggie kid lapses into unconscious denial. It's second nature to him now; lying and conning is as important to his druggie existence as sleeping and eating. He's on automatic pilot.

But slowly, insidiously, the cracks in the facade begin to show . . . first in the kid's relationship with his folks. Then his grades. Soon, he's skipped one too many practices and the coach has had it with him. His appearance is not to be believed. The grandparents can't figure out what young people are about anymore. And the neighbors think, "Oh no, not a druggie in our neighborhood." The adults are starting to wise up. But the druggie kid is so involved in his unconscious denial that he keeps right on playing the game.

DENIAL TO SELF

"I'M DOING GREAT. THERE'S NOTHING WRONG WITH ME."

A druggie's denial to himself goes something like this. A kid starts out saying he's only going to do drugs every once in a while, just a little something to keep up with Junior Jones, just so his friends will think he's an okay kid, one of the gang. That turns into, "I'm only going to smoke on weekends, and I'm only going to do pot and alcohol." When those limits start to disappear, denial begins. The fact is he is doing drugs when he said he wouldn't do them. He's doing heavier drugs than he said he would do. He's not controlling the amount of drugs he takes. And sometimes he is even overdosing. (Overdosing means loss of control of the amount of drugs used. In other words, the young person takes too much and ends up getting sick rather than euphoric because he is no longer able to judge the amount of drugs he needs for the high. The sickness may include passing out, nausea, vomiting, severe headache, speeded up or slowed down heartbeat, hot flashes, shortness of breath, respiratory failure, numbness in the limbs, etc.)

But in spite of all this, he still has a conscience. He feels guilty and ashamed. So it is important that he be able to deny to himself his use of and his need for drugs. "I can stop any time I want to but I like getting high. I do drugs because I want to, because it feels good. I don't have to do drugs."

All the while, he continues to tell himself, "I'm not in trouble with drugs." Other people may have a problem but he doesn't because he can always think of somebody who does more drugs, more often. He can deceive himself endlessly. "No sir, not me, I don't have a problem with drugs."

Druggie kids can even find "good" reasons to do drugs in their denial to themselves. Todd: "For a while I said I wanted to be a writer because I read about writers and how they could do LSD and write good poetry. And that was my justification to myself. That was why I did drugs. So I could contribute in some way."

Druggie kids who cite stories on the use of marijuana in treating glaucoma or the use of THC to prevent the nausea associated with chemotherapy ignore the stories about the harmful effects of the same substances. They use information selectively to support their denial.

This kind of denial inhibits the rational thinking that can save the druggie kid.

TYPES OF DENIAL

"THERE'S MORE THAN ONE WAY TO IGNORE PAIN."

Minimizing the Problem

It is not unusual to hear a kid on drugs say: "I don't do heroin. I don't stick needles in my arms. I don't have a drug problem." "I've only overdosed a few times and that was because I got hold of some bad drugs. The street lab screwed me up."

It seems that as long as there's somebody else around who appears to be worse off than the druggie, he can deceive himself into believing that he has not yet reached the problem stage . . . as if there is some magic line that one crosses and bells rings, sirens sound, horns honk, lights flash and "Now you are an official druggie."

The "unofficial" druggie says, "I don't do pot every day." In truth, he may have missed only one day in a month, one day of not being high, but in his own mind, that qualifies. He's not an official druggie. He hasn't gotten the gong, crossed the finish line, hit the limit.

But the limits keep changing. A kid may start off by saying, "If I had to buy them myself, I wouldn't do drugs." Or "If I have to spend my own money, I'm quitting." That can turn into, "Well, at least I don't sleep with guys to pay for my drugs. I have a job." That, in turn, becomes, "I only spend a hundred dollars a week on drugs." And so on. That's how kids maximize the minimizing.

Repressing Behavior

A child who starts out with a good relationship with his parents may be offended by the behavior of his druggie friends, so he'll promise himself, "I'll never treat my mother like that. I just won't take any drugs around her because I couldn't stand doing that to my mother." Next step: To his friends, he starts to complain about the heat he's getting from his "old lady." Onward and downward: "Shut up, you bitch, leave me alone. It's none of your business where I've been." And finally, that same child who promised never to talk back to his mother pulls a knife on her when he's high. In his mind, he hasn't changed at all. It's his mother who's changed. She started to get on his nerves. He suppresses all the feelings he has about hurting her. He swallows the pain and pushes it down far enough that he doesn't have to deal with it. He doesn't have to face and feel responsible for his own behavior—and he doesn't have to feel guilty.

This way, the druggie protects himself from more pain. "I never did that. I never hurt my parents like that. I never made a fool out of myself in front of my family and friends." It's like the person who, after a little too much to drink at the party, puts a lampshade on his head and the next day remembers being the life of the party. So it is with the druggie repressing behavior. No matter how bad his behavior becomes, he still sees it as how "cool" he was.

Explaining Trouble Away

The druggie practicing denial has an explanation for everything. If he gets busted, he says, "So what? A lot of people get busted. Possession is a misdemeanor. It's no more than a traffic ticket. It doesn't mean anything."

When the family fight starts, he says his father had a bad day at the office and had to have a drink when he got home. So he had a bad day too and needed drugs to cope.

Terry sleeps in class. He's wasted most of the time. When a teacher finally accuses him of coming to class "burnt out," he explains, "I didn't get any sleep last night. My folks were at it again. They fight all the time. I could hear them all the way up in my room, yelling at each other. They're probably going to get a divorce. I don't want them to but they probably will. It wouldn't be so bad for me but my little brother is only four. And I feel kinda responsible for him because I watch him all the time. He was real scared last night so I let him come get in bed with me. I didn't get any sleep. I'm really tired."

The teacher not only backs off from her accusation but feels enough sympathy to look the other way the next time Terry comes to class stoned. And even if she were to ask, Terry would have another excuse.

Blaming Others

Rob skipped school and got caught. It wasn't the first time and his parents were called and told. When they questioned him, he blamed it on the dean. The dean had it in for him: Four kids skipped but the dean only bothered to call his parents.

Jim worked at a fast food store. He regularly stole food and other items from the store. When he got caught, he blamed it on the store manager. "That guy is a tyrant. He never lets us take a break. If he'd let me take time for a lunch, I wouldn't take the food. He barely even gives me time to go to the bathroom."

Druggie kids can even blame other people for their violent behavior at home. Take David. He came home high regularly. His father walked in from work one afternoon and found his stoned son asleep on the couch. "Get up, you lazy good-for-nothing kid," the father yelled. David leaped up from the sofa and grabbed his father by the throat. By the time David's mother intervened, his father has already started to choke and turn red. David's explanation? "He shouldn't talk like that to me. He comes in here and acts like he can order me around. Well, he can't. I wouldn't have grabbed him if he'd treat me like a normal human being."

These are all cases of kids excusing their behavior by placing the blame on someone else. No kid blames drugs for his actions; he'd rather find a person—anyone—to pin it on.

Blanking Out Feelings

Drug use is a painful experience. Blanking out feelings, blanking out that pain is one of the ways kids con themselves.

It was Christmas day. That always meant happy times in the Sawyer household. Lots of gifts, good food and singing carols. Until the year Nick got into drugs. That year he hated Christmas. At one point, just before the family was about to sit down to dinner, Nick stormed out of the house. "He was screaming and people could hear him," his father recalls. "It was embarrassing. I mean this was Christmas day, normally a beautiful, happy, family day. This was a happy day all my life and here was my son yelling that he wanted to run away . . . on this joyous day. I felt helpless. There was no way to get my son back to smile, to sing Christmas carols and be happy. There was just no way."

NICK: "I had a lot of disappointment about that day. I was sitting in my room. I knew that I could barely stand staying in the house, not being able to get high. I was so tense that I just ran out."

MOTHER: "We didn't know Nick was using drugs. We thought it was just a teenager outburst. You know how all teenagers hate being with their families."

It is not unusual for the holidays to be characterized by family outbursts. To druggie kids, holidays represent the loss of warmth and good family memories—feelings that the druggie can no longer be part of because he has distanced himself from the rest of the family. It's an emotional time, and the druggie is likely to feel even more guilt and shame than usual. There's a sick feeling in his stomach. And the druggie doesn't know where it's coming from, so he just wants to get high to make it go away.

Emotionally charged holidays are a clue to a kid in trouble with drugs.

There's a lot of pain associated with what drugs have done to the people a druggie kid cares about—whether it's a parent, a sibling, or even a friend. Marty got his friend involved with drugs and still lives with the hurt. "It just sears all the way to my heart because if it is possible to make somebody high, I did it to him. I'd sit there and just force him, until finally he broke down. We did a tremendous amount of drugs together.

"We were lifelong friends. I had known him since fourth grade. We raised hamsters together, went fishing together. There were a lot of family ties between our parents. How could I have done that to him?"

Marty and his friend were roommates in school until the friend decided that drugs and Marty were ruining his life. He moved out. The loss of that friendship almost drove Marty to suicide. The friend went on to graduate valedictorian of his class. He stopped doing drugs on his own. Marty kept on doing drugs until he went into a drug program. But even now, clean, straight, Marty still gets teary-eyed when he talks about what he did to his friend. While it was happening, he blanked out all feelings of friendship and just looked for someone with whom he could do drugs.

How does the druggie deal with the pain that comes from holidays, the separation of close friends and the straining of family ties? He uses more drugs to help him blank out the pain.

Rationalization

With denial comes rationalization. The druggie doesn't like to deal with the fact that he can't keep his life in order, that he does things that are dumb, dangerous and illegal. So he rationalizes it away.

"I can stop using drugs any time I want to."

"I use drugs because I don't have anybody to relate to in my family."

"By the year 2000, everybody will be doing drugs."

"I do drugs because I want to, not because I have to."

"I have a job. I don't skip school. So what if I do a little drugs."

"I use dope sometimes. I'm not a druggie."

"My brother. Now there's a druggie. He does a lot more drugs than I do."

"Those kids who pass out at rock concerts, they're the ones with a drug problem."

"My folks drink all the time. They're worse off than I am. If they can drink, I can do drugs."

"I've never been arrested."

"When I have to spend my own money, I'll stop."

"I never stole anything to pay for my drugs."

Euphoric Recall

On the surface, euphoric recall looks a lot like minimizing or repressing behavior. Remember the man who had too much to drink at the party, wore the lampshade, made a fool out of himself and the next day told stories about how he was the life of the party? In minimizing, the man would say, "So I had a little too much to drink. It was a party." In repressing, he would maintain that he was the "fun guy" at the party but he would really know he made a fool out of himself. In euphoric recall, the druggie, or the drunk, in this case, only remembers the highs, not the lows. The drunk knows nothing about the hole he burned in the couch or getting sick on the rug. He only remembers the laughter, the good time. Somehow, his subconscious has magically sorted it all out for him.

Euphoric recall is like a giant mental eraser. It erases all the bad memories, the mistakes, and leaves only the good memories intact. For example, if a teenage boy goes to a rock concert with a group of friends, he gets high, loose and uninhibited. In time he gets higher and then things start to happen. He accidentally pours beer on a friend. The friend says, "Hey, cut it out." He gets defensive, angry and threatens to whip up on the friend. He gets in two more arguments with friends, continues to get higher, throws up twice, falls in a puddle, and comes close to getting in a fight with a much larger guy. The next afternoon he is with the same group of guys talking about the great time they had but when they mention his abusive temper he responds, "Come on, you guys, you have to be kidding. I was just putting you on." He'll wonder why they are making such a big deal out of it. He's not lying. That's the way he remembers it. His mental eraser has been at work. And his distorted view of what happened has become his reality.

Blackouts

Blackouts are a form of selective amnesia. Unlike euphoric recall, the user doesn't remember *anything* about certain incidents—he doesn't even remember enough to distort the events. As in a movie with all the X-rated scenes neatly edited out, the chemically dependent person snips pieces of time—hours or sometimes weeks—out of his memory. A druggie girl can get high, wake up in bed with a total stranger and have no idea where she is. A user might run into a friend who says, "When we were down at the lake, you were really spaced out. Man, you were acting strange." In fact, the drug user who has blackouts will not even remember *being* at the lake. Older alcoholics report traveling cross-country and waking up in strange cities without any idea of how they got there. But for the chemically dependent child, blackouts usually blank out hours, not days or weeks. With chronic use of either drugs or alcohol, blackouts occur more frequently and blank out longer periods of time.

HOW DO KIDS GET STARTED
"EVERYBODY'S DOING IT."

How do kids get to the point at which they have to deny the problem, to rationalize it away? How do they get from Little League baseball to big league drugs? Why would a ten- or twelve-year-old boy or girl start smoking marijuana or drinking beer? Isn't the problem all blown out of proportion anyway? Do that many kids really use drugs?

Conservative studies say that at least a third of all high school students have had enough marijuana to get high or enough alcohol to get drunk. Most high school surveys indicate that two-thirds of students have at least tried pot. Druggies will tell you that every kid they know has used drugs at least once.

In Los Angeles, undercover policemen regularly infiltrate high school ranks to try to intercept drug deals. They estimate that about sixty percent of the city's high school seniors use drugs two or three times a week and nearly a fourth of all students are stoned most of the time. "Well, no wonder," you say, "that's California." Unfortunately the National Institute of Drug Abuse says that those figures are typical of most major cities in America.

If you talk to teenagers who use drugs, what they have to say will frighten you about the reality of drug use on campuses. Most of them say they get high before they go to school every day. You heard it: *Every day. Before school.*

Sally admitted that she shot up every morning before breakfast as nonchalantly as you would admit to skipping your morning sit-ups.

Kids do drugs before school, at school, on the street corner and, yes, at home, right under your roof.

Kids are starting to try drugs at a younger age than ever before—usually somewhere around the fifth or sixth grade—and most kids are well on their way by the time they get to high school. The probability is strong that your neighbor's kids, the kids down the street, your nieces and nephews and, yes, even *your* kids, have tried drugs.

If they've even experimented, you should be concerned. Because with one high, a learning pattern develops. If it feels good once, it will feel good again. And, especially for kids, it's a lot easier to rely on that instant high than to depend on one's own internal resources to feel good.

Most kids who use drugs use alcohol and chemical substances interchangeably. If they can get the expensive, exotic stuff, they use it. If they can't, they'll guzzle cheap wine or beer. And guzzle is the right word. Druggies guzzle because the faster they consume the alcohol, the quicker they get high.

Jim has red hair and freckles. He's the kind of kid you see in a cereal commercial. He remembered his first high. "I was only twelve and was hanging out in the neighborhood with some older kids. They asked me if I wanted to get high. I said I did because I didn't want them to think I was a baby. They made me drink six beers."

Jim got high all right, and by the time he got to seventh grade, he was selling drugs at the junior high school.

Acceptance by peers has always been a powerful motivating force in the adolescent world, whether it meant wearing bobby sox or a certain kind of loafer, or learning a new dance. But listen to what kids are doing *now* to find acceptance among their peers. And remember: These are not extraordinary stories or "bad" kids.

SHARON: "I made good grades in high school. An honor roll student. I was really going for what I wanted in my future. I would go to work with my dad to learn about computers. I was interested in that. He would get books on computers for me to read. The family? I remember we used to go on vacations. We spent a lot of time together. We had a boat. I led a pretty sheltered life and was pretty secure about myself. When I started in junior high school, though, I really started feeling scared of the older kids. They intimidated me. I started feeling insecure about myself and some conflicts really started. I wanted to change my clothes style, wear jeans. I'd fight with my mom about it. I just didn't want to be self-conscious and look like a little girl anymore. I felt a need to impress other kids. So I tried using pot to impress them, but not 'til I was about fourteen. I started smoking just to be with the right crowd. I didn't want them to think, oh she's that little old-fashioned kid that clings to her mommy's apron strings.

"The first time I got high was on alcohol. I was on a double date with a druggie friend, and I got high. But I didn't like the taste of alcohol. So I started using pot, then harder drugs, to make me feel more 'in' with the people."

KIM: "I started doing drugs when I first got into high school. I guess I was always an insecure person and I wanted to be accepted. High school was neat, and everybody seemed to be getting into drugs—in the popular crowd, at least. I went with some of the athletes to the beach in a stolen car. I wanted to be accepted, and I got high for the first time that night. At first, I was embarrassed and scared. They just said, 'Do you want to get high?' and I said 'Yeah,' because I wanted to be the brave, cool one."

ANNIE: "I got involved when I was fifteen. I remember it was a lot for acceptance. I was really lonely as a kid. I never fit in. I don't ever really remember having a close friend. I could never get close to people. I used to always wonder about the cool crowd. What made them different? How come I couldn't fit in? My cousin was getting into drugs at this time, and was getting a lot of attention from the lifeguards at the beach. I was really impressed by that. I thought if I did drugs, then I would have all this attention from them, too, and I would have a lot of friends. I remember when I first smoked pot with her, I felt sneaky, and that made a sort of bond between us, against authority and our parents. It made me feel like I had a special friend. We were on the roof of a house, and I drank too much and had too much pot, and made a spectacle of myself. They laughed at me. They sat there and laughed, and I knew I still didn't have a friend. I quit for a while, but started again because I felt more insecure than ever. I thought I felt good. I just wanted attention. I got so drunk on my prom night that I spent hours sitting in a car wrapped in a blanket throwing up all over everything."

VICKY: "I started drugs when I was thirteen. I started because my friends that I hung around with got into drugs, and I just followed behind them. I thought that I would be left out or different than everybody else and I thought if I did drugs that everybody would look up to me, and I would be happy or something. I started harder drugs toward the end of the eighth grade—hash and ups and downs. I tried out for cheerleader—I thought that would be something I could do and then I would feel really good about accomplishing something for myself. But the drugs were already messing me up, and I got kicked off the cheerleading team. So I'd just go by my druggie hangout for approval and acceptance."

KEN: "I remember every night, when I was small, my mom would read a chapter out of that big, thick children's Bible. And my parents would take us on picnics and stuff. But when I got to be thirteen, I really wanted to be popular at school, and I just saw myself as looked down on. And I looked down on myself. I only had a couple of friends, and they were popular. I thought of myself as, 'Oh, nobody is going to like me, and I gotta do something so that they're gonna like me.' I was always out to make people like me 'cause I just didn't think I was a very important person."

KAREN: "I had really gotten a bad reputation in the school I had gone to before. I was known as a bop and I wanted to be a big, bad druggie, and I thought that none of my friends would hang around with me because I was going with a guy who didn't do drugs. So when we moved, I wanted to be the kind of person I had always looked up to. A tough, new image. At the first school, I felt like a freak, being straight."

Most kids who fall under the spell of drugs don't do it to hurt anybody—least of all themselves. They know it's not quite right, and they feel guilty about it from the beginning. Their parents may have never once said the word "drugs." But when a kid starts taking drugs he knows from day one that it's wrong and he does everything in his power to keep it from his parents.

Face it—drugs turn an honest, clean young person into a liar and a cheat and a thief and an emotional cripple. But everybody was doing it, right? And your kid wanted to be "in."

DRUG USE: THE DISEASE

"LOTS OF SYMPTOMS, NO CURE."

In the 1960s, the American Medical Association declared that alcoholism was a disease for which the primary treatment was abstinence from the substance. Now, the AMA has said that dependence on or habituation to a drug is also a disease. Why? Primarily because it is the catalyst for a deteriorating set of emotional, behavioral and health patterns.

A druggie can recover from the effects of drugs and live a relatively healthy life as long as he follows a health regimen that includes, first, abstinence from all mood-altering substances (alcohol included), and second, living in an emotionally healthy way, by avoiding the buildup of bad feelings. Once someone has become dependent upon mood-altering chemicals, the drug use itself becomes the primary disease. Many professionals try to treat the symptoms of the disease—emotional problems, family problems, school problems—rather than the disease itself. *It is more likely that the family problems, school problems, etc., are a result of the drug use and not the other way around.*

Beyond the emotional ramifications of drug use are the physical symptoms. Druggies have everything from the "marijuana cough" to interruption of the menstrual cycle or interference in the changes of puberty for both sexes. They are constantly susceptible to viral infections.

Ultimately, the disease of drug use is fatal. If there is no medical intervention, the only thing that follows fourth-stage drug use is death. Lots of adolescent deaths today attributed to accident, suicide, or murder are in fact drug-related deaths. Later in life, fourth-stage users die from cardiac arrest, kidney and liver failure, stroke, respiratory failure, lung cancer or a variety of other physical maladies caused by the use of drugs.

Remember, the disease started with denial. First, to others and then to themselves. And you as parents can encourage its progress with *your* denial—to others, and to yourselves.

STAGES OF DRUG USE

"DOWNHILL RACING."

Adolescent drug use goes from bad to worse in a hurry. In order to understand Kid Denial, it is important to understand how drug use escalates, the physical and emotional changes that take place and the warning signs of each stage.

Stage One

Joey was twelve. He hung around with the same three kids in the neighborhood all the time. One of the boys was thirteen and already in junior high. They had all been friends since kindergarten. They rode bikes together. They played video games together. And sometimes they got in trouble together for using their skateboards to jump over garbage cans in the street. They were a team. One summer day they sat straddling their bikes wondering what they were going to do to keep themselves entertained that day when the thirteen-year-old pulled a marijuana joint out of his pocket. The other three boys couldn't believe it. They had seen the older kids smoking marijuana. They had joked about it themselves. But they had never tried drugs. "Where did you get that?" Joey asked. "My big sister gave it to me," his friend boasted. "She and her boyfriend smoke dope all the time. Sometimes they let me smoke with them. It feels great. You guys want to try it?" The boys looked at each other, each wondering what the other thought, while the thirteen-year-old struck a match and lit the joint. He took a "toke" off it and passed it on to one of the other boys while he laughed about how great he felt. One of the boys tried it. Joey and one other boy said no, they didn't want to try it, they were afraid of getting caught. But they watched and giggled as the other two finished off the joint.

In the next few weeks, as summer vacation was winding down, there were more and more incidents like this one. The older boy showed up with pot and one by one all the boys tried it. Even Joey eventually gave in because these were his friends. They said it was fun. And they had always done things together. At first, Joey couldn't figure out what the big deal was. He didn't feel anything. But at least he didn't get caught. By the time school started, Joey was feeling it. It felt good. And still, nothing bad was happening. So whenever the thirteen-year-old could get a joint from his sister, the boys would smoke it together. Joey was a Stage One druggie.

Most kids encounter drugs many times before they actually ever take the step of trying drugs. It usually starts in a social situation, at a party or a mall or a video arcade, where there are lots of young people and lots of drugs there for the asking. Because of their moral values, most kids are able to resist for a while, but eventually, peer pressure will win out. The first toke off a joint or the first taste of alcohol usually does nothing and it will be several episodes later that a kid experiences his first high. But with that first high begins the chemical learning sequence: "I take drugs or drink alcohol and they make me feel really good. It works every time."

In Stage One, kids take drugs only when it's convenient and they're available. They only smoke pot or drink alcohol if someone else has some to share. It's like the person who says he's quit smoking, and he bums cigarettes. What he means is that he quit *buying,* not smoking. In his own mind, he's not a smoker. So it is with a kid on drugs. As long as he's not buying, he can deny to himself that he is doing drugs. Stage One kids smoke or drink on weekends and not even every weekend. Kids in Stage One drink only to get drunk and smoke only to get high. Because their tolerance is so low, it is very easy to get high on a very small quantity of substance. They guzzle beer or liquor for a quick buzz or take deep tokes off a joint of marijuana for a high. Most Stage One kids confine their intake to alcohol and marijuana, but some do get involved in sniffing glue, rush or solvents.

According to the over 2,000 kids surveyed for this book, the initial chemicals used to get high are marijuana (seventy-seven percent of those questioned), alcohol (eighteen percent) and inhalants (five percent). Nine out of ten kids say their first puffs on a joint and their first sips of beer are token moves to impress their friends. Those token puffs and sips do not result in a high or what professionals call "altered consciousness," but, under constant peer pressure, the adolescent does use drugs to the point of intoxication. That first high usually means dizziness, wooziness, loss of balance, a slight headache or distortion.

The high or intoxication or altered consciousness initiates three kinds of learning. First, the child learns to use a substance to produce a high. Second, he learns that it is easy to feel good using drugs. And third, he learns how much of a substance produces how much pleasure. That information is stored in the brain and is the basis for continued and increased use in the future.

The sequence is not unlike Pavlov's research on behavior that you read about in your college psychology textbook. Using the "reward and punishment" approach, he was able to teach rats how to run a maze. Stage One druggies are not unlike Pavlov's rats. Because their drug use is hidden from the adult world, there is no initial punishment for their behavior, only the reward of "feeling good." And the chemical learning sequence relies on kids' natural tendency to repeat whatever makes them feel good.

It's hard to spot drug use in a Stage One kid because he looks and acts normal. The only ways a parent might discover drug use during this period is by catching the child in the act— stumbling over him behind the garage, in the neighborhood passing a joint or by smelling alcohol on his breath. Some teenagers, however, might develop the personality of a druggie long before they actually get involved in drugs. Changes in types of dress, friends, language, attitude are indications of a "dry druggie"—that is, a kid who is starting to admire the druggie lifestyle. When this happens, watch out! The drugs themselves may very well not be far behind.

So, the Stage One druggie, allowed to "feel good" without consequences, progresses to Stage Two.

Stage Two

Renee is tall, red-haired, tending toward sandy blond, not really bright red. She has a fair complexion. She has a face that can twinkle but can also cloud up when she is worried or anxious.

Her father is a white-collar government worker and her mother is a schoolteacher.

The first time Renee was exposed to drugs was on a cross-country bus trip. She and a girlfriend were on their way to North Carolina for summer jobs picking tobacco. The girlfriend really painted a sophisticated, adult, cool picture of what the summer was going to be like—guys, sex, drugs, growing up. Renee started to tune in to how neat it would be to be experienced in the world, going back for her junior year of high school. Her friend offered her a drink of whiskey mixed in Coke. The two of them rode along on the bus drinking, ready for a summer of freedom.

A month later, Renee took her first toke on a joint. It didn't take long for her to become an occasional user of alcohol and marijuana. For most of her junior year, which followed the summer work experience, she drank or smoked pot whenever somebody else offered it to her. She started going to bars and rock concerts with friends, and gradually her use increased. She started buying drugs herself, thereby actively taking the initiative to get her own drugs and to get high on her own. Her schoolwork wasn't yet affected. Her home life didn't change—

things went on pretty much as usual, except that she had become an occasional drug user.

Renee made it to her senior year still using only occasionally, but with increasing regularity—most weekends, some days after school. She started using speed and Quaaludes, even experimented a few times with inhalants.

The trouble began during the summer before college. She was smoking pot occasionally but using alcohol heavily and regularly. She became sexually promiscuous. By second semester of college, her grades dropped dramatically and she had her first blackout. Now she was smoking pot four or five days a week after school. She was still living at home but she was out all night, hitting the bars. Renee was a Stage Two druggie.

It is in Stage Two that kids move from taking drugs when they're available and convenient to actively seeking them. In this stage doing drugs "feels so good" that the kid can no longer wait until the opportunity to get high presents itself. He likes the feeling so much that he begins to plan his life and his friends around getting high and he starts to buy his own drugs. This taking of the initiative is a major step in the disease.

How does the kid come up with the money to buy the drugs? Many kids still hold down jobs during Stage Two. Some use their allowances. But it is also at this point that the lying and stealing from the family to get money for drugs begin. A little money out of Dad's top drawer. A couple of bucks from Mom's purse. Then a radio, some silver, even small appliances start to disappear from the house. And that's just the beginning. As the need for drugs increases, so does the need for money to buy them.

Consumption has now gone from occasional weekend to every weekend and from several weeknights to most nights. Marijuana and alcohol still produce a high. But they reduce a kid's inhibitions, so that he wants to try more exotic drugs for higher highs. He branches out into hash, hash oil, speed (uppers) and downers. He tries sedatives and tranquilizers (if he can put his hands on them). Still, there's no real heat from home.

Early in Stage Two, the conning begins. This is what is known as the "dual lifestyle." Drugs have made it necessary for the kid to split his personality. At home, he still cares about his parents and what they think. And he cares what other adults—teachers, coaches, neighbors, grandparents—think. So he maintains his appearance, keeps up his grades in school, continues extracurricular activities and whatever else seems necessary to keep everybody off the trail. He still needs the approval of others. He still wants people to think he is straight and doing constructive things with his life.

John is the perfect example of a Stage Two druggie. "I was doing a lot of drugs but I was still able to keep self-discipline to get the grades and make the National Honor Society and Spanish National Honor Society. And I was winning a lot of geometry awards." And boy, everybody thought old John was doing great. "I had the whole school conned, my folks conned, everybody conned. And I mean I was doing a lot of drugs.

"I got to the point where I'd wear leather shoes to school and then change to my sneakers. I'd take my belt off and put it in my locker as soon as I got to school so I would go around with no belt, just to be accepted. All the druggie kids wore tennis shoes and no belts. When I got ready to go home, I'd put my leather shoes back on, put on my belt, chew some cinnamon gum, put my Visine in my eyes and things would be fine by the time I got home."

When John was with his friends, he acted like a member of the drug culture in appearance, attitude and language.

There are signs to watch for in Stage Two: Passive, withdrawn periods turn into aggressive, angry periods. Time spent alone, in a bedroom with rock music blaring (characteristic of the withdrawn period), is offset by temper tantrums and abusive language (characteristic of the aggressive period).

Also appearing in Stage Two is a lack of motivation—loss of interest in extracurricular activities, hobbies and future goals. After all, these interfere with the time a child has for recreational drug use. They require too much effort and planning. And given the choice of feeling good because he's made the swim team or feeling good from taking drugs, the kid already controlled by the chemical learning sequence will opt for drugs. It's easier and faster.

It is also during Stage Two that a kid no longer needs friends to get high. Now he will sometimes get high alone. The peer pressure that introduced him to drugs has given way to his own need to be high.

In Stage One, a kid takes drugs to feel good. By the time he reaches Stage Two, he also uses drugs to self-medicate. That is, he uses drugs to make himself feel good when he feels bad. So drugs have become a way of dealing with the low blows in life. When this happens, drug use is past the point of being merely recreational. Drugs have become a coping mechanism.

The Stage One druggie denies his drug use to others. But the Stage Two druggie starts to deny his drug use to himself.

Parents tend to avoid taking any action in Stage Two. They know something is wrong but it's not bad enough to tackle yet and they can still dismiss many of the changes as growing pains. If they nag the kid about school, he will straighten up— but it's only temporary.

For the druggie kid, the increasing loss of control over his drug use, the changes in personality, playing the dual lifestyle roles all spark a series of internal conflicts that are emotionally painful, confusing and frightening. And you know what comes next, right? More drugs to make the pain go away. Stage Three.

Stage Three

By the time the kid reaches this stage, getting high has become the most important thing in his life. He uses drugs to feel good and to avoid bad feelings. He gets high almost every day and either goes to school already high or gets high at school, much like the alcoholic who drinks on the job, first at lunchtime, then on coffee breaks and eventually keeps a bottle in his locker or desk drawer. He is losing his ability to cope with stress, disappointment, fear and other everyday emotional difficulties.

Although marijuana and alcohol are the mainstay drugs, the

kid moves onward and upward to harder drugs: LSD, cocaine, PCP or PHP (angel dust), THC, MDA, opium, mescaline, etc. The use of uppers and downers increases. Use changes from regular weeknight to regular weekday use. By the end of Stage Three, the druggie kid is high most of the time. And he gets high alone more often than with friends.

Because of the kid's increased tolerance, it takes more drugs, more often, to produce the same high. The first overdose usually occurs in Stage Three, resulting in vomiting, blackouts, numbness, unconsciousness, nervousness, and screaming . . . and sometimes death.

The kid in Stage Three drops all Stage Two pretenses of being straight. He associates openly with druggie friends. He is no longer interested in pleasing parents or teachers or any other adults. He's only interested in getting high. Regular weekday use has grown to include use before and during school.

Now it's too difficult to maintain the dual lifestyle. The druggie kid would rather use the energy that it takes to keep his parents in the dark to find new ways to get high. Being sneaky takes time and effort. The Stage Three druggie is no longer willing to put that time and energy into a front. By now, he'll say, "Yeah, Mom, I use drugs. All kids do drugs. That's where it's at today, Mom. You're so old-fashioned. You don't know anything about what things are like now. There's nothing wrong with doing drugs. I'm not going to quit."

If a father gets mad because his son is bringing around friends whom he considers a bad influence, and he forbids the boy to associate with them anymore, the Stage Three druggie's response will likely be, "Hey, Dad, I use all the same drugs they do. You might as well leave them alone because I'm just like they are. Don't you understand? We all do drugs. You think there's something wrong with them. Well, there's not. The only one there's anything wrong with around here is you."

Stage Three is the "who cares what parents or anybody else thinks" stage.

His dress is no longer dual lifestyle, changing clothes when he leaves the house. Now marijuana leaf T-shirts, coke spoons on necklaces and drug buckles are a more familiar part of the wardrobe than loafers and preppie shirts. Straight kids are dropped from his circle of friends. He gives up all pretense of liking school. He skips school regularly and his grades have gone from dropping to failing. School, jobs or anything that might get in the way of doing drugs are out.

Because still more drugs are needed to produce the desired high, more money to buy drugs is needed and so crime increases. More stealing from parents. And stealing moves to the public arena, friends and strangers. The druggie usually has his first contact with the police in Stage Three, after breaking and entering, running away, stealing cars or shoplifting.

Jeff was such a druggie. He grew up in an affluent family. His father was a successful businessman, heading several companies. His parents were divorced. Jeff stayed with his mother most of the time. When he was fourteen, visiting his father in New York, he wanted to be accepted by the new friends he met, so he started doing alcohol and smoked his first joint. When he went back to his mother's, he continued to drink and to smoke pot, and he moved on to harder drugs. By the time he was in the ninth grade, Jeff was smoking pot every day, five or six joints a day. He was also doing speed, cocaine, downs and opium. Occasionally he experimented with acid.

He got kicked out of school. And when he was fifteen, he stole his father's car. He was picked up in West Virginia and spent a week in a juvenile detention center. Jeff's dad's idea of putting his foot down was to place him in a strict private school. But Jeff continued to use drugs regularly and got in more trouble. He shoplifted, stole money from his parents and was involved in several breaking and entering capers with friends. He would sneak out of the house in the middle of the night and take his mother's car.

When Jeff began literally pushing his mother around, she kicked him out of the house. He lived with a druggie friend until he was kicked out of there too. By the time he was seventeen, Jeff was getting high all day and sleeping in the street or on people's lawns.

Another of the downhill fast patterns that appears in Stage Three is drug dealing. Remember: more tolerance, more drugs, more crime to get drugs. The kid who deals buys larger supplies of drugs and in turn sells them to friends to pay for his own supply.

Kids know who has drugs to sell. They can tell by the seller's dress style and behavior. Most kids maintain they can go to any strange part of town, a strange city even, and find any drug they want in thirty minutes—just because they know who to stop on the street and where to make a deal.

Drugs are as readily available on school campuses as they are on the street. And it is the Stage Three druggie doing the deals. Nick: "It was easier to get LSD at my junior high school than it was to buy a bottle of wine on the street." With dealing, however, comes a lot of associated crimes, more contact with the police and more fear.

Watch for the physical signs of a Stage Three Druggie: A constant cough, red eyes, sore throats and fatigue. The marijuana cough sounds much like the chain smoker's cough. Teenagers in Stage Three are subject to more than the usual number of colds and viruses and bouts with bronchitis.

The highs are now accompanied by strong lows. "Coming down" causes intense depression. The criminal behavior elicits powerful feelings of guilt. The kid's relationship with the family has totally disintegrated—there is no longer any close physical or verbal communication, just physical violence and verbal abuse. And that causes more pain. The druggie kid suppresses all his feelings and just does more and more drugs to make it go away. Now he's self-medicating, taking more drugs to deal with the pain caused by his own drug use. He feels worthless, different from everybody else. He sees everybody else as happy and comfortable while he hurts. He thinks he's going crazy. All this pain adds up to his feeling that his life isn't worth living. The guilt and pain and sense of going crazy chip away at his feelings of self-worth ("I am a piece of crap"). Overdosing and thoughts of suicide are frequent.

In short, the Stage Three druggie not only loses control of his drug use but he loses control of everything in his life. He can't obey laws. He can't finish any activity. His attention span decreases. He starts to speak in short, inarticulate sentences. He can't handle complex ideas. He can't hold a job—either he gets fired or quits. He either quits school or skips until he gets suspended. He gets caught for dealing or possession. He starts running away from home. Casual sex turns into promiscuity, often including bizarre sexual behavior, group sex or homosexual activity.

He becomes careless in his use of drugs and often leaves paraphernalia and drugs in open view, crying for help to make the pain stop. Next? Stage Four.

Stage Four

This is the final stage of drug use. Beyond Stage Four is death.

The kid who has advanced to this stage uses drugs not just on weekends, not just on weeknights, not just weekdays, not just before school and at school, but excessively and compulsively *All the Time.* He no longer uses drugs to feel good. Now he uses drugs to feel normal.

The druggie kid in Stage Four stumbles out of bed in the morning and has to get high immediately just to function. Pain is now associated with the drugs. But the druggie kid can't stop.

It is in Stage Four that kids may turn from "taking" drugs to "shooting up" drugs. Shooting up is a term usually associated with heroin, but kids can shoot up Quaaludes, Valium, speed, cocaine, PCP, THC and Dilaudid (a painkiller). Dilaudid, Quaaludes, Valium and speed usually come in pill form. Cocaine, PCP, and THC come in powder form. In order to shoot up these substances, the drug must first be changed to a liquid form. Kids do this by mashing the pills into a powder (or taking the powder itself when the drugs comes in that form), mixing it with water and heating them together to melt the powder down —most often by putting the mixture in a spoon and holding it over a match or candle. The liquid is then put into a hypodermic needle and shot into the vein. Heroin is used in the same manner.

Why do druggies start to shoot up? Because this is the most efficient way to get high: The drug goes directly into the bloodstream, moves more quickly to the brain and causes a more immediate high. Drugs that are swallowed go into the system through the lining of the stomach. Drugs that are snorted go through the lining of the nose or the walls of the lungs. Marijuana, of course, goes through the lungs. But marijuana to the Stage Four druggie is like water to a gourmet. He won't turn it down, but it is incidental to the many and varied more potent substances he uses to get high.

The Stage Four druggie can no longer distinguish between normal and high. The street term for this is "burnout," which manifests itself in zombielike behavior. The kid appears wasted all the time, his eyes are glazed, dull, his movements slow. He has lost and continues to lose weight, his memory is weak, and he is coughing a lot. School, jobs and family relationships are out of the question. The moral values he began relinquishing at the end of Stage Two aren't relevant anymore, because he can no longer even distinguish between acceptable and unacceptable behavior.

Many kids at this stage turn to prostitution to support their drug use. Sarah was such a case. She would walk the street at night, stopping cars, offering men either intercourse or oral sex for twenty dollars. With two or three customers a night, she had enough money to get through the next day's drug use—and then it would start all over again.

Sarah must have come from a troubled, lower-class family, right? *Wrong.* Sarah was a "nice" girl from a middle-class family in Ohio. But when the rest of her friends were going off to college, she decided to take some time off and travel. She had already learned about drugs and she liked the feelings. College didn't fit. It all started innocently enough, drinking bottle after bottle of cough syrup to get high from the codeine. But that turned into painkillers. And that turned into shooting up. Expensive. Sarah told her family she was working as a waitress. Instead, she was dancing topless in a bar.

Most of the girls she worked with were there for the same reason—money for drugs. So when men started offering Sarah money for sex, it was an easy step to make—easy in the sense that it was an easy way to get money, which meant getting high, an "easy" way to feel good—but not an easy step to make psychologically. Sarah painfully recalls her first "trick." "I was nervous. It was three years ago but I remember exactly what he looked like. He was about sixty years old. He said he was a veterinarian. He wrote down the address of a motel and told me to meet him there after work. I parked my car in the motel garage. I remember going past the desk and into the elevator and feeling like it wasn't really me. 'I can't believe I'm doing this.' I don't think I told him it was my first time. But I remember knocking on the door and waiting in the hall and still not believing I was really doing it. I went into the room and I didn't know whether to act aggressive, take my clothes off or what. I got the money first and put it away. I really didn't know what I was doing at all. I was really naive. But I remember when I left the room, got back on the elevator and went to my car, I felt really different." Eventually, having sex for money seemed a lot easier than dancing in a topless bar for four hours a night and two hours in the afternoon, so she danced less and turned more tricks until eventually full-time prostitution paid for her drugs and her druggie lifestyle.

Often, drugs cause kids to get confused about their sexual identities. Such was the case with Sarah. She was only eighteen but because she had sex with men for money, the only close sexual relationship she developed was with her female roommate, also a druggie and also a prostitute.

They had sex, bought drugs, had more sex and bought more drugs. Then they found a doctor who would give them drugs in exchange for sex or for watching the two of them have sex together.

Soon, Sarah was shooting up Dilaudids every day before breakfast. She was having sex with the police chief just to keep the cops off her back. Eventually she was caught robbing a drugstore—not for money, but for drugs. She was ordered by the court to enter a drug rehabilitation program.

In Stage Four, thoughts of or attempts at suicide are more frequent. There is more pain. In this stage, the highs, the excitement, the good feelings have all given way to chronic emotional pain.

In Stage Four, drug use has become a terminal disease.

ESCALATION OF DRUG USE

"THE HIGHER THE HIGHS, THE LOWER THE LOWS."

Now you can see how denial allows a kid to continue drug use until there is virtually no turning back. That's why it is vital that you as parents look *not only* for drugs and drug paraphernalia but also for *signs* of drug use in your child. Don't let him deny—to you or to himself. Intervene as soon as you spot the first signs. You don't want to hear stories like these from your kid, do you?

ADAM: "I O.D.'d on speed at school and they thought it was pot. I had taken a bunch of speed before P.E. because I thought it would help me run. The coach said I was lazy and I wanted to show him. I started getting all kinds of rushes and then I started getting sick and throwing up blood."

DAWN: "My folks were hassling me so I ran away from home and went to Daytona Beach, Florida. This guy met me on the boardwalk and asked me if I wanted to be a model. So I started doing nude modeling for him. He would have sex with me and I would get drunk and pass out a lot. I got tired of it and ran away. Then I met up with this other guy on the street. He asked me if I wanted to get high with him and I said I did. I got in the car with him and he pulled a gun on me. He walked me to the woods and he was going to rape me. But he didn't have to use the gun. I didn't care. You can't rape somebody who's willing.

I thought of jumping in the river and killing myself just so people could see my body washing up on shore."

KYLE: "I thought I had gotten a girl pregnant when I was fourteen. She was thirteen. I had sex with her in the woods behind the school. And I did a lot of twisted things with sex . . . maybe two or three guys with one girl. I was on drugs all the time I did it. It was an everyday thing for me, getting high and looking for sex."

KEVIN: "I was about fourteen and I was down at the beach with my friends. There's where we went a lot to get high. We were just there and having a good time and I was feeling good and then this guy asked me to take my clothes off. I didn't know what was going on. I just did it. He started putting his hands all over my body and then I figured out what was happening. I was scared but I was so high that I didn't know how to stop it."

CHRIS: "I was really a bitch in school. I would throw things at the teachers, call them names, tell them to shut up. I started doing weird sexual things. After I got suspended five or six times, they were going to kick me out of school for good. I couldn't talk to my parents. I didn't have any boyfriends. Everybody just used me for my drugs. I tried running away but that didn't work. So I thought I'd kill myself. I thought about it a lot. That was going to be my big escape. I thought it would be exciting, see the blood, things like that. I went downstairs and got a knife, and I started slicing my arm and it was bleeding. I thought this is really neat . . . then I saw my mom's sweater lying on the chair and I started to wipe the blood all over her sweater to get even with her. Then it started hurting and I got scared. I went back upstairs and bandaged myself up."

KEVIN: "When we moved, I really started going to big parties and doing a lot of stuff. I was really scared of it for a while, especially PCP, because I had seen on "Sixty Minutes" where people jumped out of windows and stuff like that. Then I did PCP one time and it didn't make me crazy. So slowly I just got into more and more drugs. I wanted to be the guy who always had the drugs. I was buying my friendships. I started spending a hundred dollars a week on just drugs. There were times I thought I was going crazy and I used to ask myself, 'What's wrong with me, why is everything going wrong?' I never tried suicide but I would get on my motorcycle and pass cars in the median strip, crazy things like that. I would be going ninety miles an hour and sometimes I would feel just like moving over that center line in front of a big truck. That would be a good way to go."

LISA: "It was hailing and snowing in Virginia. I had had on the same clothes for three days because I had been sleeping with my druggie boyfriend in an abandoned shack. I was freezing. My boyfriend had hit me and I was drunk and scared. I was only thirteen. We got in the car and we're tearing down this icy road. First we hit a car and then we crashed off the road into a ditch. Another girl got out of the car, her braces had gone through her lip and she walked over and hit me. I wandered over to the road and started hitchhiking. Some guy stopped and picked me up. He was married but I went off with him. I didn't have regular sex with him but I had oral sex."

PAT: "I was only sixteen. I had already run away from home. I was living with this divorced guy. And I got pregnant. One day I went horseback riding and I got thrown. The horse stepped on my face and then he stepped on my stomach. I went back to the apartment and I laid down because I was swollen and bleeding and I was starting to have cramps really bad. I thought I was losing the baby so I called the guy at work and he didn't even care. He wouldn't even come home. I was in a lot of pain. . . . finally, I miscarried. . . . I flushed the baby down the toilet. Then I really got high. I was lying on the couch with my face all bruised up. I had just lost my baby and I started to think about killing myself. I knew there was a gun in the apartment. I went in and I got it and I was going to shoot myself

. . . going to blow my brains out . . . so he'd have to come home and see my brains splattered all over the bedroom. The only thing that kept me from pulling the trigger was I caught sight of myself in the mirror, my hand was really shaking and I just couldn't do it. So I just stayed high for two days. When I finally ran out of drugs, I went to the doctor to see what was wrong because I was still bleeding."

None of these kids ever stopped to consider that perhaps it was the drugs that were screwing up their lives.

Now that you have had an intimate look—perhaps more intimate than you were prepared for—into the druggie's mind and life, remember that none of these kids were "bad" kids *before* drugs. Now they are kids with bad problems. They are caught up in the self-perpetuating cycle of hurt and self-medication to stop the hurt. With this process comes family explosion, arrests, horrible behavior and pain for everyone. But somehow the pain never hurts enough to make the kid acknowledge drugs as the cause. For the kid, drugs are still the painkiller. And that's Kid Denial.

Kid Denial Checklist

1. *Does your child have abrupt mood changes for no apparent reason? Do you pass this off as "puberty"?*
2. *Does your child seem moody, depressed, withdrawn?*
3. *Does your child have new friends whom he won't bring home or who don't seem to fit your family's style?*
4. *Is your child avoiding the family and spending a lot of time alone while at home?*
5. *Has your child suddenly lost interest in some really important hobby, sport or activity?*
6. *Does your child seem argumentative or rebellious? Is the conflict between your child and his siblings becoming a problem?*
7. *Are you suddenly having problems controlling your child?*
8. *Is your child late coming home? Is he evasive about the where and when plans? Is he sullen and private or rebellious about his privacy?*
9. *Are your child's grades dropping? Are you getting calls about conduct problems at school?*
10. *Has your child stayed out all night?*
11. *Has your child's attitude toward school changed, with talk of dropping out, of not needing school to be successful?*
12. *Has your child's appearance (clothes, hairstyle, make-up and jewelry) become a central issue in family arguments?*
13. *Has your child skipped school or classes?*
14. *Does your child have health problems such as a hacking cough, persistent acne, weight loss, colds or other infections?*
15. *Has your child ever run away from home, or threatened to do so?*

3

Family Infection
"Show me a druggie kid and I'll show you a family in pain."

Bert started doing drugs when he was eleven. By the time he was fourteen, he was getting his younger sister Kate high. She was only twelve. She started blowing marijuana smoke in the face of her two-year-old brother Sean to get him high. She and her friends even got the family parakeet high. Their father tried to be their "buddy," hoping that would cure the problem. But their mother just couldn't take it anymore and left home, alone, four months pregnant with nowhere to go.

This is a family in pain.

Families are systems, with family members woven together like threads in a fine fabric. Each family member has a stake in the others, and when something goes wrong with any one of them, the repercussions, often profound, are felt by everyone. The system is shaken. The fabric has a defect. And every member of the family would rather deny, compensate or run from it—anything but face it and deal with it.

The popular notion today is to look for a flaw in the family fabric as the reason for the kid's drug use. Did Mom work? Was Dad out of town too much? Did he miss all the special events, like birthdays, recitals or Little League games? Was the smart big sister too much competition? Did not making the debate team cause the problem? Well, listen up: None of these things will cause a kid to get involved with drugs.

Of the 3000 cases we studied, introduction by an elder sibling was the most common cause for a child's first experiment with drugs. The second largest contributing factor was the child's involvement in a peer group where drugs were considered to be "cool." Way behind these two was a family member's (parent's or grandparent's) chemical dependence on alcohol or another drug—not as a genetic issue but as an issue of family climate, a learning pattern that is being subconsciously passed on. And the fourth contributing factor was a child's physical or mental impairment (being a slow learner, having a kidney ailment, etc.) which led him to resort to drugs so that he could feel like one of the gang.

There is no common denominator among families with a kid on drugs. The problem would be a lot simpler if there were. There are just as many druggie kids who come from two-parent homes as there are from single-parent homes. Remember: *Family problems, in and of themselves, do not cause a kid to do drugs, but family problems can begin as a result of a kid on drugs.*

Listen to Bert's mother talk about what drugs did to her family: "Things were so out of hand with Bert when he was fourteen that I really thought he was insane. He had been doing drugs for several years. I was trying to be tough with him. But his father wanted to be the good guy and let him do what he wanted. He just wanted to please him. I felt I had to be the strength. But things went so far that I was past being in control of him or his mind. And I was afraid for myself.

"I was about three months pregnant and I was spending a lot of sleepless nights. Every time I'd hear a sound I was scared to death he was going into Sean's room and hurting him.

"It seemed like we got into arguments all the time for no reason. He would grab me by the arm and push me against the wall. Once he grabbed me at the top of the stairs and tried to throw me down the stairs. I really was afraid of him all the time.

"It got to the point where there was so much arguing and fighting in the house that I could see I was playing Kate off of him a lot. She was only thirteen but I would go to her for approval when I punished Bert or restricted him. I had no idea she was using drugs. And I wanted her to tell me I was doing the right thing, that I wasn't being too hard on him.

"My husband and I would disagree over how to handle the situation. I was desperately looking for some kind of facility that would take my son because I couldn't take it anymore and my husband wasn't helping. I finally put Bert in a private hospital that has a drug program for kids. His dad and I both knew it was drugs.

"I just wanted to get rid of him. I wanted him out of my life. Then Kate started going way out and she overdosed a couple of times. She had started to yell at me. She told me to go away. She didn't want to hear my problems.

"When Bert came home from the hospital, things were good for a few days. And then it started all over again. Things were just like they were before he left. Now I had two yelling, abusive kids and I really didn't know what to do. I was even more scared. I told Bert to get out of the house. He left.

"The next day he came home. When he knocked on the door, I was afraid to let him in. I told him I wouldn't let him in until his dad came home. I had a friend there visiting and Bert started trying to kick the door down so I let him in. But I told him to just get his clothes and leave. He did but he yelled obscenities at me the whole time.

"Three nights later he came back in the middle of the night. It was cold and snowing and my husband let him in. In the morning he told me Bert was back and I asked him why he had let him in. He said, 'What else could I do? Let him stay outside and freeze to death?' And I said, 'What about me? What about the baby? I'm afraid he's going to kill us!'

"We argued about it and finally I said, 'If you're not going to make him leave, I'm leaving.' And I just got in the car and started driving. I drove all the way from Virginia to Georgia. I hadn't eaten or slept. I checked into a motel. Then I started spotting and having contractions. I had to call a doctor. He told me to just stay in bed a few days or I was going to lose the baby.

"There I was in a motel room. I only had the clothes I had grabbed before I ran out of the house. I had even left my two-year-old with his father. I was scared. So I waited for a few days and then drove back home.

"As soon as I got home, Bert started to threaten me again. And Sean couldn't be left alone anytime, even in his own room. He would be sitting just calmly watching television, then he'd just jump up and start yelling. He would run into his room and get under the bed. He kept crying, 'They always yell at me. They always yell at me.' I didn't find out until later that Bert and Kate had been taking him downstairs and getting him high. He was scared to death of them. That's when I decided if I wasn't going to lose the baby and if Sean wasn't going to go completely berserk, and if I couldn't live with the fear of Bert getting up in the middle of the night and killing us all, I had to leave. So I did. I resented it a lot because I felt like my husband chose two druggie kids over me."

This story may seem bizarre. The family may seem mad. But in fact this family is not so different from the hundreds, indeed, thousands, of drug war-torn families in America.

A kid starts on drugs in the fifth grade. He gets high for three years and then turns on his younger sister. She gave her younger brother his first high when he was two. And even the parakeet? Kate: "We put pot seeds in his bird feed. My friends and I would sit around and blow smoke in his cage. Then we'd take him out and let him try to fly. He'd flutter all over the place and bang into walls and things. My friends thought it was hilarious."

And what did the parents do? Just what a lot of parents do. They went to their corners and came out fighting. You see, parents usually react to drugs in the family in one of two ways —either by trying to nurture it away or by withdrawing from it. It's the divide-and-conquer strategy. One parent becomes the Caretaker. The other shrinks away from it and becomes the Withdrawing Parent. And kids go right on getting high.

THE CARETAKER PARENT

"I WON'T LET THEM STOP YOU FROM DOING DRUGS."

Being the Caretaker Parent grows out of normal parenting. It has to do with taking care of kids, loving them through thick and thin, nursing them through pains and ills. But the Caretaker Parent also expends a lot of energy and emotional effort in pretending the problem doesn't exist (Parent Denial) and cleaning up the drug messes the child leaves in his path at school, in the neighborhood, with the police and at home. The Caretaker Parent makes him or herself crazy trying to convince the other parent, other kids in the family and outsiders that there's nothing wrong. It's all he can do to keep the kid in school and out of jail and keep the other parent from closing in, being too stern, too strict and shutting down the kid's act.

In some cases both parents may become Caretakers. Working together in the name of family self-respect, they try to make it all better. But in most cases, there is only one Caretaker Parent and he or she will hold onto that role at any cost. In fact, sometimes the Caretaker Parent will devote so much time to worrying about the druggie kid, getting him out of trouble and keeping the family afloat that he or she will end up getting fired from work. Maintaining the family status quo is the number one goal of the Caretaker. And that goal inevitably becomes blinding—to the needs of the druggie kid, to the rest of the family and even to the Caretaker's own needs.

THE WITHDRAWING PARENT

"GET ME OUT OF HERE. THIS HURTS."

The Withdrawing Parent is the one who is "mad as hell and is not going to take it anymore." Because of the pain, the hurt, the anger, the turmoil that rages around him or her, the Withdrawing Parent throws in the towel early and says to the Caretaker, "Okay, so you want to be in charge. You got it. I give up."

Withdrawing may not mean going as far as Bert and Kate's mother—physically withdrawing from the family. There are many different kinds of withdrawal. Leaving the house is just a physical manifestation of what Withdrawing Parents do in a variety of ways every day. There's the parent who withdraws to the newspaper, never taking his nose out long enough to acknowledge the fight going on in the living room. Or the parent who withdraws into television. Or golf. Or the basement to do woodworking or sewing. Withdrawing can be anything, so long as it allows the parent to say, "I'm out of this one" and pass the baton to the Caretaker Parent, who is always willing to cope with and clean up the mess.

When faced with the choice between a druggie kid and a frantic family, even parents who had never liked their jobs will end up choosing work. First, there will be later hours at the office. Then weekends. Then trips out of town. Then *lots* of trips out of town.

The Withdrawing Parent looks for other ways to feel good. The family is causing too much pain. And if the pleasure doesn't come from work, the Withdrawing Parent may turn to an affair or a series of affairs to feel better. He or she becomes convinced that the Caretaker Parent is involved in a conspiracy with the druggie kid, always taking up for him, never laying down the law and so he or she feels rejected by, alienated from the spouse. Remember how much Bert and Kate's mother resented it that her husband "chose two druggie kids over me." To fill that void, the Withdrawing Parent looks for love and attention somewhere else. Of course, the ultimate form of withdrawing is the parent who packs up, walks out and seeks a divorce, saying to himself and to the family, "I don't like the pain. I have needs too. I'm getting out of here." That *really* leaves the Caretaker Parent holding the bag. But the Withdrawing Parent can rationalize that away with, "You say you can fix everything, well just go ahead, you live with it, you take it, you listen to it, I'm not going to."

The Caretaker or the Withdrawing Parent may end up turning to chemical substances for relief—usually alcohol, but sometimes drugs. In order to deal with the enormous stress and pain of trying to keep the family together, the Caretaker parent may turn to tranquilizers. Seeking refuge from the family storm, the Withdrawing Parent may turn to alcohol.

Either parent may agree to take all the blame for what's going on in the family. You see, one of the things chemically dependent people are good at is convincing people who are not chemically dependent that there's really something wrong with THEM. It's not the least bit unusual to hear the wife of an alcoholic say, "My husband says I'm crazy and I think he's right. I feel like I'm going crazy." Of course, the fact is she is not going crazy, but her world has gotten crazy around her *because* of her alcoholic husband. The same thing applies to parents of druggie kids. The kids start doing crazy things and tell the parents it's all their fault. The parent may end up at a psychiatrist's or family counselor's office saying, "I must be having a nervous breakdown because I just can't cope." It's not the parent who's out of control, it's the situation.

But often it seems as if the parent has entered an unwritten pact with the druggie kid: "I'm crazy. It's not your fault. I must be the reason you're having all these troubles. I'm sorry I'm doing this to you." The parent may end up going for treatment or even checking into a mental ward just to be able finally to pinpoint what's wrong in the family. "Blame me," he says. The seeking of psychological counseling—whether it be a trip to a therapist or commitment to a mental ward—becomes both a physical and a mental escape hatch for the parent *and* the child.

THE FAMILY DRAMA
"WHAT PART ARE YOU PLAYING?"

The parents aren't the only ones in the family suffering, changing roles and altering lifestyles to accommodate the druggie.

A human system is a group of people with common interests, working toward common goals through common means. If any member alters the system and other family members don't understand it or approve of it, chaos, pain, frustration, fear and anguish result.

Remember what we said about families being systems. Think of the mobile. Each part of the mobile has its own shape, balance and space. But all the parts are hooked together by a series of sticks and strings. In a family, those sticks and strings are feelings, relationships one to another, rules and expectations. That's what holds families together.

So when something happens to any member of the family, any part of the mobile, every other member, every other part of the mobile has to spin around and shift and twirl to find a new balance.

A child leaves home, goes off to college, everybody adjusts. Dad changes jobs, everybody shifts. Mom decides to go back to college, everybody gets new responsibilities. There's a birth in the family or a death, everybody's affected. Everybody shifts, shakes and compensates to make the family mobile find its new equilibrium.

So when one member of the family has a drug problem it's no surprise that the rest of the family mobile is shaken. At first, the changes are small, almost imperceptible, and so the moves to compensate are subtle. Family members may not know what the problem is, they just know something is different and they start doing their part to balance things again. Change occurs. Everybody responds.

When the druggie kid starts to create problems at home, everybody changes behavior. Parents start to give the child more time and attention to clear up the trouble. Brothers and sisters start to stay out of the way, to give the druggie kid "his space." The trouble at school starts, things start to disappear at home, explosive family fights begin and everybody has to find new ways to weather the storm.

The new behavior turns into role-playing, with each family member wearing a mask. The mask allows each person to act out his new role, providing a facade behind which to hide from the hurt, anger, disappointment—all the feelings that belong to the real family member role.

Each family member acts out whatever he perceives his new role to be. But there's no director, no play, no script, no lines for this new drama. Everybody ad-libs. That makes for very bad theater. And rotten real life.

When family relationships turn into role-playing, then everybody in the family has been infected by the drug disease.

So we now know that the parent masks are those of a Caretaker and a Withdrawing Parent. But what happens to the brothers and sisters of the druggie? How do they adjust? How do they find new balance? What masks do they don?

THE SECOND USER

"IT LOOKS GOOD FROM WHERE I SIT."

Tragically, one of the most common decisions a druggie's sibling may make is to join the druggie brother or sister and become the Second User in the family. The Second User role grows out of a feeling of admiration. The primary user, usually the *older* brother or sister, looks "cool." He has lots of friends. He always appears to be having a good time. He's daring and independent. It all looks pretty good from where the Second User sits, so *he* tries drugs: "My brother John is really jerking my parents around. They jump up and down and do anything he wants. He gets more freedom all the time. He looks cool and together and he's having a good time."

Physically, the Second User has no problem getting into the chemical learning sequence—take drugs, feel good—because drugs are available right under his roof. And remember that the druggie brother or sister has a high stake in keeping the Second User on drugs—that way he can make sure there are no tatt-letales in the family.

Think back to Bert and Kate. It was Bert, *not* an outsider, who got Kate involved in drugs. Kate was a good student. But because she was "a good kid," her mother leaned on her. She got a lot of attention but it wasn't the kind she was looking for. When she brought home her report card, her mother would say, "Oh, that's good, honey. Now would you go out behind the house in the woods and see if Bert is back there getting high?"

It was also Kate to whom Mom turned for advice. Because she tried to be strict and lay down the law, she wanted some-body to tell her she was doing the right thing, that she wasn't being too hard on Bert and that it was for his own good. When her husband wouldn't provide that endorsement, she turned to her good daughter. At home, Kate was her mother's angel. Away from home, things were different.

"I started hanging around with his friends, wearing real tight jeans and acting real druggie. I was only twelve but I was going to this scummy bar."

Before long Kate was doing pot, hash, speed, quaaludes, prescriptions, nitrous oxide, cocaine, acid and PCP. She had her first overdose from taking "a handful of pills" and was taken to the hospital before she turned thirteen. "I don't know what they were."

Kate seemed pretty straight to her parents. She kept her grades up. But in reality she was hiding behind her mother's need for her support, playing the game just to perpetuate her mother's belief—"Kate is really straight. I can depend on her."

When her mother left, Kate said it really hurt inside but she wouldn't admit it. Instead, she just thought about how she was going to be able to get high at home while her dad was at work. Her friends would think that was *really* cool. It would be like having her own place—all that freedom! But she kept looking for attention.

"I had a lot of different boyfriends, a different one every

month. I tried to get the ones who were dealing and stuff like that. I just used them to get drugs. It didn't make any difference if I liked him or if he were cute or anything, just so he had drugs.

"I was hitchhiking one time and this guy stopped to pick me up. He was about twenty-four. And he asked me if I wanted to go to a motel room and get high. He had hash. So I went to the motel with him. We got high, and I went to bed with him."

The Second User protects his own use by sympathizing with his parents. He encourages them to focus on the problems of the primary user to keep them off his back and leave him free to do all the drugs he pleases.

Parent Denial is particularly strong with a Second User. After all, parents need one child they can hold up to the rest of the world to prove that they're good as parents. "Suzie is such a good girl. I don't know what we'd do without her," they say to their friends. "At least we did okay with her," is what they say to themselves. Having more than one child on drugs is more than a parent's feelings of self-worth can handle. Parental denial is the best protection the Second User has.

All goes well for the Second User—everybody buys his con until the moment of crisis. The crisis is usually a series of events that force open the eyes of the denying parent. Imagine, for example, that in one week Suzie gets kicked out of school, arrested for shoplifting and overdoses. The parents may have managed to ignore any one of these events but three in a row makes them sit up and take notice. Wouldn't the parents with the experience of the first child detect the problems with a second child more quickly? No. The parents are so busy monitoring the gradual changes in a primary user that they usually miss the warning signs in the Second User. Their obsession acts as blinders.

Unfortunately, drugs do not always stop with the Second User. Sometimes, drug use dominoes through an entire family. Listen to Alex: "Everybody in my family except my little sister did drugs. It really took a toll on us. It ruined the whole family." Alex is eighteen. He did pot, alcohol, hash, hash oil, THC, LSD, PCP, MDA, crystal meth, ups, downs, prescriptions, Quaaludes, speed, cocaine, opium, mushrooms and mescaline. He had two brothers and one sister who were also on drugs. One of his brothers died when he jumped from an eighteenth-story window after taking LSD. Did it make the other kids stop and think? Did it make them get straight?

ALEX: "I even went to his funeral high. The next day I was out snorting cocaine and doing drugs. And it must have been three weeks later after he died of LSD that I was doing LSD again."

So Second Users can turn into thirds and fourths. And the family "fabric" continues to unravel. So parents, take warning: The first and most prevalent response of younger siblings to a druggie in the family is to become a Second User.

SUPERKID TO THE RESCUE

"FASTER THAN A SPEEDING BULLET . . . CAN BEND STEEL WITH HIS BARE HANDS."

Superkid is usually, but not always, the oldest child in the family. It is this child who makes good grades, is constantly achieving and about whom everybody has nice things to say.

So when the crunch comes and the family crisis starts, it is Superkid to the rescue. He or she will try to offset all the bad that is going on by a Herculean effort to excel in all endeavors.

Superkid sees a lot of pain and hurt in the family and says, "This is not for me. It's horrible. It's embarrassing. It's hurtful. It doesn't fit into my picture of the perfect life. I've got to do something to make it different." And so he sets out to create a whole new world of super accomplishments.

Superkid is the family hero, someone to rally around. Superkid sympathizes with the parents and may even sometimes act as a third parent, taking charge of problems. Superkid is the one who has to go along on those trips to the police station to claim the druggie brother or sister or the one who has to keep an eye on the problem kid. Superkid wants to make things better for the parents and the family.

Teachers and ministers and coaches can't say enough good things about Superkid. "I know you must really be proud." Or, "I wish I had a son or daughter like yours." Or, "You don't find many kids like that these days. You sure are lucky." So Superkid is used to getting strokes for his achievements. But all this isn't easy for Superkid. He can often get stretched out too far, trying to be all things to all people. The pressure to perform, to keep the family face, can become too much for him—because no matter how much this kid does—scholarships, academic awards, star of the football team, chief cheerleader, homecoming queen, head of the church youth group—it's not going to make the family pain go away. It may bring some temporary accolades, some family esteem, into the picture, but it doesn't stop the hurt for long and that leaves Superkid stressed and more pressured than ever. He is tense and generally dissatisfied with himself for his inability to solve all the problems. And no amount of achievement can make Superkid feel good about himself. Why? Because the message of being worthwhile has to come from the family, this fragile network of people who are so busy hurting and feeling inadequate because of a chemically dependent child that they can't make anybody else feel worthwhile. And anyway, who'd figure Superkid needed it?

Superkid often creates a fantasy about his family, one more in harmony with his perfect picture. Superkid keeps his friends away from the house because he doesn't want anybody to know that his family isn't perfect. Dates, even best friends, aren't allowed to come home with Superkid. He doesn't like to share the pain of the trouble at home with others—better that other people see his home life as an episode straight out of "Ozzie and Harriet." Teachers, coaches, friends, would all say that Superkid's family epitomizes the best of American family life, because that's the way Superkid portrays it.

VICKY: "Marlene really disappointed me. I told her that I had my ideas of a perfect family and she blew it. I didn't want to publicize the fact that we didn't have the perfect family, either.

My teachers thought I was the best kid going, they really loved me, and they couldn't believe Marlene was my sister.

"I didn't know what a druggie looked like or acted like. So I really couldn't tell until she got arrested. . . . Marlene ran away seven times. We were at church one night after this luau kind of thing and my mother told me to watch Marlene. I was sitting with my friends, and I turned around and she was just gone. She was like that. She disappeared right out from under my nose. She did that twice. Another time, my mom was out of the house and she told me to watch Marlene. I was in the family room watching television and she was up in Mom's room watching television. Then I went back there and she was gone again. I was supposed to look after her, but I wasn't supposed to tell her, 'I'm watching you.' Because I was the oldest and I didn't have a big mouth like my younger sisters, my mother would talk to me because she knew I wouldn't tell Marlene.

"My friends and I were considered the cream of the crop. I'd go to school, practice swimming for three hours a day, then go home and do homework.

"But in the summer all I can remember is Marlene was always missing. We'd get up really early on Saturday morning to look for her. My dad would come in and wake me up, then he and I would get in the car and search for her. We looked everywhere. My dad even did some breaking and entering trying to find her in some druggie's house. My dad was really paranoid after a while. For weeks, my whole life just revolved around looking for Marlene. We didn't do anything else but look for her. And the whole time I was out there I was growing to hate her more and more because she was robbing me—robbing my whole family—we were falling apart because she was doing what she called 'being free.'

"I hated the fact that I couldn't say, 'Here's my perfect family, isn't it wonderful?'

"When she'd come home, everybody would make a big deal out of it and treat her really special. And I felt like Marlene was a druggie and being rewarded for being home and just doing what I'd done all my life.

"But I had to support my mother, regardless. I'd do that anyway because my mother really needed me when Marlene was gone. It really ruined her. I had to prove to her that no matter how bad Marlene was that I was still her daughter and I would always do good things and support her."

Tragically, no matter how hard Superkid works, no matter how much he or she achieves, the druggie kid always manages to ruin it.

Vicky: "When I had swimming meets, my whole family would show up, my parents, my sisters, even Marlene, but I didn't trust her. If my event was coming up, I'd be constantly looking around to see where she was. Even though the rest of the family was there, I still felt like I had to keep an eye on her. My mind was always sidetracked."

ANOTHER SUPERKID: "I was always the do-gooder. I wanted to keep everything going fine. I didn't want fights or anything. So I tried to keep everything calm. If Carol didn't do her chores, I'd do extra, hers and mine, just to keep everything peaceful.

"I play the violin. I'm into trombone at school. I'm in all advanced classes. I do everything. I play basketball. I fit in with people. I get along with other people real easily. I get along with teachers because I like teachers. I like to learn. I really resented Carol. I had to give up a lot of stuff because of her. I was very embarrassed . . . like at school. If somebody would say something bad about my sister, I'd yell at them, 'You're wrong, there's nothing wrong with my sister. My sister's great.' But I would never bring friends home.

"What Carol did to me was every time we'd get ready to go to one of my recitals or something, there'd always be a fight. Just before we were ready to leave the house, she'd say she wasn't going. She'd say she didn't have anything to wear. She didn't want to go. She'd stand right at the front door until Mom would have to physically jerk her in the car, just pull her out to the street and throw her into the car, so she would go. And then, I would usually mess up because I would get so nervous, wondering what my sister was doing and thinking she never really cared."

Superkid provides his parents with an endorsement of their parenting abilities. Thanks to Superkid, parents can say to themselves, "Well, we must not be too bad or Susie wouldn't be making straight As or John wouldn't be quarterback of the football team and make all-conference. We must be doing something right."

THE BAD ASS

"YOU CAN BLAME ME. DOES THAT HELP?"

Along comes another kid in the family that is frantically trying to clean up the druggie messes. This kid looks at Superkid and says, "No way, I'll never be able to measure up to that." He keeps waving his hand, saying, "Look at me. Here I am. I need love and attention too."

Superkid is older, smarter, more experienced—in general, more attractive. The Bad Ass can't possibly top that by doing more Superkid stuff. So he looks around and, seeing all the attention the druggie kid is getting, decides that the easiest way to get attention is to imitate the druggie kid. And even if he never actually gets involved in drugs, he can do everything but. So he starts to hang around with a different crowd, the bad kids. He starts to get bad grades, skip school. He does some shoplifting. Pretty soon everybody at home is yelling at him too. Success! He has the attention he wanted.

This takes the focus off the druggie kid and allows him to go at breakneck speed into more and harder drugs. Now the Bad Ass Kid is taking the rap for the trouble at home. Everybody feels good that at last they've gotten to the root of the problem. "Ah-ha. There's hurt and pain in this family and you're the reason for it." Not the druggie, no siree. It's the Bad Ass Kid.

The outwardly rebellious one. He's the problem. Since Bad Ass is getting the attention, that encourages more bad behavior, *more* negative attention. The druggie couldn't be happier to have the Bad Ass Kid around. And who knows? The Bad Ass may very well eventually get into drugs himself.

THE FAMILY CLOWN

"COULD I HAVE JUST ONE LITTLE SMILE, PLEASE?"

Sometimes there is another kid in the family—often the youngest—who tries to steal some of the attention from the druggie by becoming the Family Clown.

Every time this kid looks up there's another emotional bomb going off in the family. A little tiny kid looks at all those big angry people, throwing things, yelling at each other, hitting, and he says to himself, "I don't like this stuff." He tries to find some way to defuse the bomb, either by performing or being cute or cuddly.

The Family Clown is a barometer in the family drug storm, constantly on the storm watch, waiting for any cloud or clap of thunder that will send him into action. It is he who provides the distraction and amusement for the family in pain.

But being the Family Clown is not happy work. The Family Clown lives every day afraid that he won't see a family cloud or that he will see it too late. The Family Clown suffers daily the pangs of confusion and anxiety—confusion because he doesn't know what's going on in the family and anxiety because he is constantly waiting for the next family explosion. He's always wondering what's going to happen. Family Clowns are often given to ulcers and other kinds of nervous disorders as a result of living with the stress of trying to keep the family laughing.

Doug is six. He's the Family Clown. "I would draw my mom pictures all the time. I would make her lots of happy faces with smiles on them to make her laugh. But I'd get scared when I went to bed. I always had nightmares about my sister and her druggie friends coming into the house, stealing things, trying to hurt me or something."

Tracy was only five when she learned to be the Family Clown. "My mother would make these rules and then my brother would come in around twelve o'clock at night and they'd start yelling. He used to kick holes in the pantry door and things like that. I'd get out of bed and go out there. I'd tell him he was making Mom sad and I didn't like it. I didn't know what was wrong with him. I just didn't want him to be mad. I'd try to make him laugh. I'd do the Cookie Monster and E.T.'s voice or something so he'd quit making my mom cry."

THE PASSIVE KID

"GET ME OUT OF HERE."

In the middle of all this family ruckus, there may be one sibling who can't stand all the fuss, all the activity, all of the volatile emotional stuff. This is the Passive Kid. Driven nuts by all the static in the family, he deals with it by simply shutting it out, withdrawing to his own place and into his own mind. This is the kid about whom outsiders and the rest of the family will say, "Isn't Sally nice? She's so quiet."

The Passive Kid does not join in any of the turmoil, never gets in trouble and performs well in school. He's used to being patted on the head.

But the Passive Kid never really feels in touch with everybody else because he spends so much time hiding, either physically or psychologically, from the rest of the family. He usually withdraws to his room, to read, watch television, draw, or paint.

Vicky's youngest sister, Cindy, is a Passive Kid. Cindy starts to cry when she talks about what she did to get away from Marlene and the family problems. "I'd normally go to my room and just do things in my room. Play with my Barbie dolls, things like that. I just did things with myself. I'd watch TV or play with my stuffed animals. I would just play fun things. I could hear them but I wouldn't think about it."

Marlene was hiding drugs under Cindy's mattress because she knew that no one would think to look in Cindy's room.

Even though the Passive Kid usually makes good grades, he may appear vacant, distant when you talk to him, almost as though he's tuned in to something else and not listening at all. The Passive Kid is also likely to hide in his own fantasy world.

MARGARET: "Everybody would start to argue and I'd just leave the room. I didn't want to face the fact that my family was having a problem. I'd listen to music, put on my headphones so I could shut out all the noise."

KIM: "One time we had to tie up my sister because we had to take her to a mental hospital, she was getting so crazy. She told me if I didn't cut her loose, she would kill me. And I was just watching and crying. I didn't know what to do.

"It was always so embarrassing. You know, if the windows were open and the air conditioners weren't on, everybody could hear all the talking and screaming.

"When I found out she was on drugs, I didn't really care because she had hurt me so much. She used to bring these druggie guys over and she'd do things with them and she'd make me watch.

"I was ten. And I was always afraid of them because they would beat me. My sister and her druggie friends would come up to the window at night when I had my pajamas on and watch me.

"My sister would do things and blame them on me and I just took it because it was easier to take the blame than to take the beating I would get from her and her friends later. I would just go to my room and pretend I was some kind of rich person or something. Or I'd pretend I was in England, away from my family, and I was the princess's maid or something. I had a lot of daydreams and stuff like that. Sometimes I imagined I won a million dollars and what I'd buy. My family was never in my daydreams. They were always about a whole other place and whole different people.

"Sometimes I would pretend I was on this big, puffy white cloud with a big nine on the side. I always wondered why people would say 'cloud nine,' so I'd imagine one. It was quiet and nothing was there, you know, just me. Nobody was yelling at me or telling me what to do. It was just quiet and peaceful.

"I had started to think my family was normal. I thought every family screamed and yelled and threw tables all the time. But then again, when I went to Catholic school, I thought everybody in the world was Catholic too."

The Passive Kid's tendency to internalize stress may lead to high blood pressure, or stomach, kidney or heart problems. If stress is held in, it will express itself physically somewhere in the body.

KIM: "I felt under a lot of pressure all the time. I'd get lots of headaches. I even started getting real bad dandruff and the dermatologist said it came from stress."

So the Passive Kid's cloud nine may not be as safe as it looks. The Passive Kid feels enraged that he is alone and withdrawn from the pain and turmoil of his family. He's distant and hostile but the hostility never surfaces. He appears "nice," shy and somewhat apprehensive. Passive Kids can also withdraw into drugs. And, of course, the final withdrawal is suicide. The Passive Kid may tell the whole family that he can't take the hurt, the pain, the emotional noise anymore by removing himself from the situation. Permanently.

Of all the sibling roles, the two who are most likely to survive the druggie family are Superkid and the Family Clown. That is not to say that they will walk away unscathed, but they do walk away with the fewest scars visible to the untrained eye.

Superkid will survive because he has developed his own set of achievement skills which he can use outside the family. But it is also Superkid who has the most difficulty realizing he has a problem, that the druggie in the family has had an impact on his life. He defends himself by pointing the finger. "You think there's something wrong with me. Look at the rest of you. I'm successful. There's nothing wrong with me."

The problems that Superkid will hit in his life will have to do with making effective connections with other human beings because of his avoidance. As an adult, Superkid is the one who will become a workaholic, be very successful at what he does, be admired in the community, but may have a difficult time finding a satisfying marital relationship. Superkid may go through life expecting his spouse to be a cheerleader for his accomplishments. And he expects the accomplishments themselves to be enough of a contribution to the relationship.

The other survivor is the Family Clown, who will likely go through life telling jokes, being adorable and making people laugh. As an adult, that behavior might begin to look immature. But the Family Clown has learned that making people laugh is a way of not dealing with reality. So the adult clown may also have a hard time having an honest relationship or marriage because he is used to avoiding problems rather than dealing with them. People only make emotional connections if they can face and deal with differences between people. The Family Clown might also have problems as an adult with the hard work and seriousness needed to achieve academic or job success.

The Passive Kid is the one parents should be most concerned about because in the family turmoil, the quiet Passive Kid can get lost. Passive children plod quietly through life as loners, feeling disconnected from other people. They have tendencies toward depression and suicide. And if the Passive Kid chooses drugs as a way of withdrawing, it can be very dangerous.

The dangerous thing about all the roles people assume in a druggie family is that the mask hides who the person really is, thus hiding the true feelings, true needs and true vulnerability. Each role is a defense mechanism to protect the role-player from the pain surrounding him. It's a means of coping. Some people have called it "frozen feelings."

When feelings are hidden, communication dies. Human beings lose touch with each other because nobody can decide what parts belong to the role and what parts belong to the real person, which feelings are real, which just a smokescreen.

Family communication is essential. People in a family are supposed to know each other, understand each other, care about each other and love each other. All that adds up to a family's self-worth as a whole and to an individual's self-worth as an individual human being.

When the druggie forces a family into manning the battle-fronts, grabbing drama masks and assuming new roles, family self-worth and individual self-worth deteriorate. Individual survival takes over. It's every man, woman and child for himself, trying to survive in a hazardous, threatening, painful situation. Selfish survival becomes the rule. Nobody has the energy to help another person because so much energy is being spent taking care of one's own survival needs. All behavior becomes defensive.

Even Superkid can't stand it when he looks around and, with all his achievements, his family is *still* in shambles. He worked so hard and the family self-esteem is gone. He has his trophies, but he's lost the family of his dreams.

During Stage One and the early part of Stage Two of the druggie's use, the family is not likely to make any visible changes. Family members don't see the problem so they don't have to find any new behavior to compensate. The druggie kid has started recreational use to feel good but the family mobile is still perfectly balanced.

When the druggie kid starts to self-medicate to feel good in the middle of Stage Two, his behavior subtly starts to change. He is still in control of his personal behavior but he has started to con his family to protect his newfound drug pleasures. As the druggie's mood and attitude start to change at home, the family mobile gets it first nudge, and family members start to swing around looking for a new, safe place to hang. Soon the acid rock music gets louder. The druggie starts to stay in his room with the door closed. And then the sudden bursts of anger begin. The family starts to feel uncomfortable. And now everybody has to adjust.

At first, family members don't know what to do so they may try out a number of different defensive behaviors. A parent may try being a "buddy" to the druggie child. Or the parent may agree to buy the druggie child a horse or a dirt bike—anything that might appease him and improve the family communications. Siblings will test their limits with the druggie to redefine the relationship.

When family members start to try out these new roles, the family drug disease process has begun. Remember, all family members are tied together by a series of experiences and emotions. And if one family member starts to change, everyone else changes, too.

When the real trouble starts—trouble at school, trouble with the police, explosive family fights, abuse of siblings, dropping out of outside activities—the family is forced to deal with the changed druggie kid. Family members still don't know that drugs are the problem, they just know a problem exists and they have to cope with it. So every family member grabs a mask and adopts a new, accommodating behavior. One parent will start to withdraw from the family. Another will start to protect the druggie kid and become a Caretaker. Other kids in the family grab roles. They start to copy the behavior of the user and get involved with drugs or Bad Ass Kids and Family Clowns start to act out a new role to deflect and dilute the family furor. Superkid will strive to build family self-esteem outside the home. Or an older kid may leave home, get a job and find his own self-esteem. Meanwhile, the disease is spreading, communication's dying and family relationships are changing.

When the family situation turns into a raging storm, family members become desperate just trying to survive. The Caretaking Parent becomes compulsive about cleaning up the druggie kid's messes and taking the blame for his behavior. The Withdrawing Parent no longer just disappears into a book or a project—now he's away from home constantly, especially when trouble is brewing.

Superkid is striving for success, constantly seeking and conquering new territory and trying to do everything perfectly. Bad Ass is now well on his way as a druggie himself. The Family Clown is sad and hurting inside. The Passive Kid has emotionally removed himself from the family. Behaviors have become compulsive and defensive, as everyone struggles to survive in an impossible, painful situation.

If the new defensive roles fail, people start to jump ship, hoping to hit life rafts. The Caretaker Parent, having failed at making things better, will either join the kid in his chemical use —drugs or alcohol—or end up volunteering to be mentally ill just to have somebody else take care of him for a while. The Withdrawing Parent may simply walk out on the whole situation in an angry reaction to the relationship between the druggie kid and the Caretaker Parent. Superkid has discovered a way to get out on his own, leaving the Caretaker Parent with the user, the Second User, and a withdrawn, depressed Passive Kid or a sad Family Clown.

If there are only two children in a family, the sibling combination will most likely be a User and a Second User, a User and a Superkid or a User and a Bad Ass. The User–Passive Kid combination could occur. The User–Family Clown combination is the least likely. When there are three children in a family, the most likely combination is the User–Second User–Superkid. The second most likely combination is User–Superkid–Bad Ass. It is possible to have three users, but there is usually one child who feels responsible and tries to make it better for the parents. The Family Clown is most likely to show up in families with more than two children.

Family Infection Checklist

1. Have your family members started to feel uncomfortable or uneasy with each other? Are people being cautious with each other?
2. Do you feel that you are not quite in touch with other members of the family?
3. Are there family secrets, that is, do some people conspire with kids to cover up things?
4. Are one kid's problems becoming a battleground in your couple relationship?
5. Is one kid's behavior becoming the focus of the family?
6. Stop for a minute and think: Is there a child in the family who is so withdrawn and quiet that she is never a problem?
7. Are there family alliances where a parent and child will team up against the other parent?
8. Does your family feel as though it is out of control, as though you are reacting to things after the fact, rather than really making decisions ahead of time?
9. Does your family have a child who gets attention by (a) bad behavior or (b) clowning behavior?
10. Is there another kid in your family who is a super achiever but conveys false impressions about the family to outsiders?
11. Are you or your spouse starting to avoid the heat at home by working, travel, clubs or hobbies?
12. Are you and your spouse really together on handling the kids, including rules and consequences?
13. Is there a kid in the family who is acting like an extra parent, making up for someone's absence?
14. Is the problem kid starting to run the family?

4

Parent Enabling
"Let me help you hurt yourself."

A young couple sat in their beach apartment smoking pot. They had used marijuana regularly since college. They were part of the antiwar movement in the sixties. They talked a lot about peace and love. And they got stoned.

In some ways, their lives are really different now. He's a stockbroker. She's a college professor. They have a two-year-old daughter. They've become part of what they used to protest against—mainstream America. They come home from work every day and instead of having a drink, they light up a joint. They do it to unwind. They consider marijuana less harmful than alcohol. And just so their little girl doesn't feel left out, they bought her a bubble pipe so that she can play pretend with them while they smoke their pot pipe.

Hard core, huh? Bet you're not going to be surprised that that little girl may very well be using pot and several other drugs in a few years. And you probably think it will serve those

94

parents right if they end up with a kid who has a drug problem. After all, they're encouraging her to do drugs, right? They're enabling her. Well, don't be so quick to judge. The chances are if you're a parent, you do a little enabling of your own. Oh, granted, it's probably not so obvious as our stockbroker couple. But it's enabling, nonetheless.

Chances are you do it every day. Chances are you don't realize it. And chances are it's just as dangerous as buying a child a bubble pipe. Maybe even *more* dangerous.

There are all kinds of enabling and all kinds of excuses. The father who comes home and mixes a double scotch and water is enabling. He says he needs it, business is terrible. It helps him unwind. He doesn't think he's enabling. But the truth is, he's just as much an enabler as the sixties couple. He just doesn't know it.

A fifteen-year-old girl who had been doing drugs for three years said she "mostly" did pot, and she didn't see anything wrong with it. When she was asked why, she said that the first pot she ever saw she found in her mother's bedroom. Her parents were divorced and her mother was dating a state senator. He would bring the pot over and he and her mother would get high in the bedroom together. If a state senator did it . . . if her own mother did it, it must not be so bad. Again, parent enabling.

Most parents can understand that doing drugs or alcohol themselves is enabling their children, encouraging them to do drugs and alcohol. But the part of enabling that parents can't understand is the insidiously destructive "help" they give their children. Getting a kid out of trouble, for example, may seem like helping but may actually be enabling.

Sometimes, in an effort to be understanding, parents are actually enablers. For example, the parent who doesn't like the friends a child brings home, doesn't like the trouble his kid is getting into at school, doesn't like the havoc he's causing at home—and does nothing about it—is an enabler. Parents need to realize the difference between real helping and enabling, real understanding and enabling and real support and enabling. Enabling is reflexive. Parents do it without thinking. It is as natural a part of being a parent as conception and child-birth. It starts when a child is born and continues throughout the parent-child relationship. It is the helping hand that parents extend to their children throughout life. Because parents love their children, they support them. They care about them. They enable them.

In the very early years, parents let small fingers cling to strong hands while toddlers get their confidence and strength to walk alone. They stand a few feet away with outstretched arms and say, "come to Mommy" or "come to Daddy." Soon that child is ready for his first two-wheeler and parents run alongside the bike while the child wobbles his way, finding his balance. By being that helping hand, parents save skinned knees and bent-up bike frames. But more than that, they are saying to a child, "I'm here. I'm supporting you."

And so it goes in the parent-child relationship. Parents are always enabling their children. They enable them to have hob-bies, get an education, learn to drive a car, get a job, buy a horse. Enabling is something parents feel good about. It's a part of nurturing. It's helping prepare kids for the world they live in.

Helping a son make a down payment on his first home for his family is something to feel good about. Helping finance a daughter's decision to go back to school and get a law degree is something to feel good about. But when it comes to a child experimenting with or using drugs, enabling is nothing to feel good about. It's dangerous.

The basic learning behavior for a child is "if you do some-thing and it hurts, don't do it again." Or "if you do something that feels good, do it again." When parents keep small fingers out of electrical outlets or keep small hands from reaching up and pulling pans off the stove, they are protecting the child from pain—intervening, *not* enabling. When parents intercede in a child's drug use, they are taking away most of the pain. Parents stop kids from paying the price for their drug use. The small child gets a slapped hand instead of boiling water spilled on him, but the druggie child gets no pain of punishment and no pain from his behavior. So he continues to take drugs to feel good. Parents who intercede in a kid's drug use and do a cross-body block to prevent him from suffering the consequences of his behavior are enabling—hurting, not helping.

It is absolutely imperative for you as a parent to learn about enabling. There is little question "if" a parent is guilty of en-abling because, like Parent Denial, Parent Enabling is second nature, and it is done in the name of loving, caring and support-ing. But if you continue to enable a druggie kid, you may as well be selling him the drugs.

How do parents enable their children to do drugs? Take a look at some examples.

A mother was shopping with her fourteen-year-old daughter. The daughter asked for some money. When the mother asked what she was buying, the daughter showed her a bong, an apparatus used for smoking marijuana. The mother immedi-ately wrote a check for twenty-six dollars. Why not? She thought it was a bud vase! The mother was naive, uninformed and an unconscious enabler.

Jim was caught stealing money from the pizza house where he worked on weekends. The money he earned wasn't enough to buy all the drugs he was using so he started stealing money from the cash register. First it was a couple of one-dollar bills, then fives, then tens. The management let the stealing continue until they had an iron-clad case against Jim, and then they called the police. Jim's parents were called down to the station house to face their son and the pizza house owners. The police explained the situation to them. Jim was only sixteen, too young, his parents felt, to face the consequences of his actions. Instead, they offered to pay all the money back to the pizza house, along with a little reward, if the owners would just agree to drop the whole matter. The police advised some sort of juvenile probation for Jim, but the parents thought that was too heavy-handed. They paid off the pizza house owners, put their arms around their son and drove him home. They gave him a good lecture on honesty, but they never questioned him on what he was doing with all the money he had been stealing. By "cleaning up" Jim's behavior—righting his wrong—and not making him face the consequences of his actions, they enabled him.

When Mrs. Murphy was cleaning her son's room and noticed a label on some of his recording equipment that said "Hillboro County Schools," she talked her husband into wrapping the equipment in plastic and returning it to the school late one night while the school was closed. They didn't want their son to get caught, so he didn't have to face the pain, and they didn't have to face the embarrassment. They were enabling.

After Joann was kicked out of school for selling drugs her senior year, her mother tried to get the school to take her back. But they demurred. She had already been kicked out of two other schools. Her mother wanted her to get away from the "bad" kids who were getting her in trouble. The mother ended up spending $60,000 to get Joann into the only school that would accept her—in Switzerland. All Joann needed was the freedom to do more drugs! Joann's mother sure spent a lot of money enabling her daughter.

There are all degrees of enabling—everything from the parent who talked a teacher into a passing grade for his child to the parent who lied to the cops when they wanted to know where Liz was at 2:00 A.M. Friday. "She was upstairs asleep," the Enabling Parent said. "Are you sure?" the cop questioned. "Of course, I'm sure. You think I don't know where my own daughter is at two o'clock in the morning?"

Or the father who bought his son a third car after the boy had already totaled two cars. Or the mother who agreed to sign twenty-eight absentee slips in one semester without doing something about it. Or the parents who moved from Maine to Florida and agreed to take their son's marijuana plants in the moving van. Or the grandmother who got talked into watering her grandson's marijuana plants because he told her they were Japanese tomato plants. She kept watering, turning the plant in the light, fertilizing and wondering why she wasn't getting any fruit for her efforts. No Japanese tomatoes in sight. But you can be sure her grandson kept the plants well pruned.

There are two kinds of Parent Enabling behaviors. The first is parent behavior that gives kids the message that it's okay to do drugs. The second is parent behavior that makes it easier for kids to do drugs by protecting them from the negative consequences of their drug use.

Parents often get *trapped* in enabling behavior when they have a child on drugs. They know drugs are the problem, and they try bargaining as a way of keeping the kid under control. For example, a divorced mother worried that her son was doing drugs because there was no male disciplinarian in the house. She knew that her son felt cheated and she felt sorry for a teenage boy with no male role model at home. She was worried what might happen to him if he continued to stay out late at night drinking and getting high, so she made a deal with him: If he were going to smoke marijuana anyway, at least he could do it at home where he was safe. So her son started bringing his friends over and pretty soon his room became a marijuana den. The mother thought she was keeping her son safe by letting him smoke at home. Instead, she was saying to him, "Drugs are okay, if you do them at home."

The same thing happened when a father got tired of his son stumbling home drunk in the wee hours of the morning. The father had visions of his son ending up splattered all over the highway or in the emergency room, so he agreed to let his son drink at home *if* he would promise not to drink away from home. He even agreed to let him use the refrigerator in the basement to store his own beer. The message? "Alcohol is okay."

A lawyer in a suburban area of Denver found out the hard way. He and his wife decided to give their son a "keg party" for his eighteenth birthday to celebrate the boy's coming of age. There were lots of teenagers at the party, among them three girls who lost control of their car on the way home and hit a tree. All three were killed. The parents of the three girls sued the lawyer for allowing their underage daughters to drink alcohol. The parents won the case and the court's judgment against the lawyer was so immense (in excess of $10,000,000) that the family was ruined. Over the next year and a half, the lawyer lost a significant number of clients. The emotional impact of community sanction exacerbated his problems, along with those of his wife and children, and he finally gave up, stopped practicing law, sold his house, and moved his family to a "hiding place" in the mountains. Pretty stiff consequences for being a good-guy parent and providing a keg for his son's friends, wouldn't you say?

The second form of enabling parent behavior is taking away negative consequences. If the child never has to face his behavior, he only remembers the part of drugs that feels good—not the consequences of his behavior that feel bad. As a result, the child believes drugs are all good because he experiences all of the pleasures and none of the pain associated with drug use.

As long as parents are permissive about druggie behavior, as long as kids continue to press the limits without negative results, kids will continue to use drugs. When enabling stops, drug use does not necessarily stop, but when a parent stops saying it's okay, he is one step closer to realizing the whole situation is out of control, and it's time to do something about it.

What does it take to get a parent to stop enabling? It may take a trip to the police station or the emergency room. But waiting for a crisis to happen to stop enabling is like playing with a loaded gun.

The mother who did nothing when she realized that her son had used her bank card at an automatic teller to make seven withdrawals, for a total of $250 within a twenty-four-hour period, was waiting for a crisis. The father who put out $750 in legal fees to get his son off a charge of grand theft auto when he knew his son was guilty was waiting for a bigger crisis. So was the father who, after learning that his daughter was sneaking out of the house at night to get high, took a psychologist's advice and spent $25,000 to build another room onto the house, so that she would have her own separate entrance to go and come as she pleased. Even that father can look back on the situation now and wonder how he could have been so stupid. At the time, he thought he was doing something really special for his daughter that would make her understand how much he loved and cared for her. It was not until she was arrested for prostitution that he stopped enabling her to do drugs.

THE MOTIVATION

"DOING WHAT COMES NATURALLY."

We've talked about how enabling represents good intentions. But you know what the road to hell is paved with. Extended family members, neighbors and friends will be impressed by the contortions that you put yourself through to "help" your child. But are what they see as loving and caring heroic efforts on your part *really* loving? Is it really loving to allow your child to continue something that may threaten his life? Is it really loving to stop him from suffering the consequences of his actions?

And what about the motivation? Is *that* truly loving and caring? Or do you fix up, clean up and cover up out of a fear of embarrassment? Would having a kid kicked out of school and put in jail be more than you could handle with your friends and family? Are you afraid people are starting to wonder what kind of parent you are if you let your child get into all this trouble? Is saving face more important than saving your child from drugs?

But think about it for a minute: Even if your enabling grows out of loving and caring, is it any less lethal than enabling that grows out of selfishness and embarrassment? No. Sadly, enabling is all too often good love with bad results.

VARIETIES OF ENABLING

"How can i hurt you, let me count the ways."

Ignoring Behavior

The first and most obvious kind of enabling is ignoring behavior. When a child first starts to get in trouble at school, when grades start to drop, a parent's first response is to pretend there is no change and hope it will go away. When the child begins to get sassy at home, talk back to parents and fight with siblings, parents choose first to ignore it. But when a child's feelings and behavior are changing because of drugs, ignoring it isn't going to make it go away. The situation will only deteriorate as drug use continues. And the drug use will be allowed to continue only if the parent ignores the situation and does nothing to change it. And we're back to another self-perpetuating cycle.

The Peterson family had always been close. Their only daughter had plenty of friends and was a good student. Then things started to change. "We had all the signs," her father recalled. "Her schoolwork suffered, her habits changed, her extracurricular activities dropped. But we didn't think anything about drugs because we didn't know anything about them. She had been doing pot and alcohol for about a year. Then she started mixing quaaludes and alcohol.

"She got in a car accident with some friends and she tried to hide it from us. She called and said she was going to stay over at a friend's house. But I could tell by her voice that she was upset. So I insisted she come home. I knew something was wrong but when she walked in the house, there she was all banged up, all gashed up with blood all over her face.

"Turns out she had skipped school with some other kids who were dropouts. I checked out the kids she was with and found out they were doing drugs. When I checked at school, I found out she had been cutting classes regularly. [She had missed forty-three out of forty-five schooldays.] We still didn't associate her behavior with drugs. We didn't think she was doing drugs even if she was with other kids who did. I even talked the school into forgiving and forgetting if she could come back."

Hiding Behavior From the Other Parent

Parents employ this type of enabling because the nurturing, caring, protective parent likes to befriend the child and keep the stern, disciplinarian parent from discovering what's really going on.

The Petersons were guilty of this one too. First, both of them joined together in laying down the law. They set curfews. They checked to see if their daughter went to school. And there was absolutely no going out on school nights.

Then one night their daughter announced that she was going out anyway. Mrs. Peterson stood her ground. "Oh, no, you're not, young lady. You're not leaving this house." Mr. Peterson intervened and told his wife to leave the room, he'd reason with his daughter. After all, he had always been the one who was able to handle her. But their daughter walked out, leaving them both angry, hurt and speechless.

Mrs. Peterson recalled the evening. "I thought I was going to lose him. He was like Rhett Butler. It was so dramatic. He went into his bathroom and stayed locked in there for hours. He was just emotionally unhinged."

MR. PETERSON: "She had always done pretty much as I wanted her to. Yeah, I was a mass of emotions because I knew I was losing control of her."

That incident became the dividing line in the family. From then on, Mr. Peterson was afraid to tell his wife all the trouble that their daughter was in—partly because he didn't want to upset her, and also because he was afraid of the family altercations that would result.

Then came the day that Mr. Peterson came home from work early and found a strange car in the garage. He didn't think that much about it. When he walked in the house, he found his daughter in bed with a man. "This guy was a pusher and she had apparently been getting her drugs from him. I came close to sticking a knife in him. I didn't tell my wife anything about it. I didn't want her to know. And I told Ann I wouldn't tell her mother. I thought her mother was too abrupt, too argumentative. The two of them always argued back and forth."

Some parents hide things from the other parent to protect the child. Like the mother who smelled alcohol on her son's breath when he came home from school and told him he'd better brush his teeth and gargle before his father came home. Often the conscious motivation is to protect the spouse—like the mother who says she won't tell the child's father this time because Dad is having a particularly hard time at the office right now and it wouldn't be fair to bother him with the problem. But the parent who hides drug behavior from another parent is giving the same "okay" message to the child as the parent who says it's okay to smoke marijuana at home. Fighting drug use and drug behavior requires a unified parental front. Hiding behavior from a parent, whether in the name of peace or protection, is enabling.

Why? Because the parent who agrees to hide something from the other parent is in effect naming him or herself a co-conspirator in the kid's drug use. He is joining the drug team and playing opposite the other parent. It may feel right because you are now closer to your troubled child than anyone else. But your participation on the wrong team will inevitably produce a disastrous last quarter.

Accepting the Blame

Parents would rather blame themselves than blame their children for doing drugs. It's convenient to have a hook to hang drugs on. Working parents, divorced parents, low-income parents, high-income parents can all look at their child's using drugs and say, "It's all my fault. If we hadn't both been so intent on our careers . . . if we had made the marriage work

. . . if we could have given our child more opportunities . . . if we hadn't given him so much. . . ." The druggie kid loves these games. Now he has the perfect excuse to do anything he wants. If you, the parent, will buy the ticket, you can bet he'll go to the game and win. You've given him all the strategy he needs.

Well, listen up:

No matter how nasty the divorce, no matter how severe the learning disability, no matter how traumatic the childhood illness, there are always other kids with the same problems who do not do drugs. Those kids manage to deal with their problems in far more constructive ways.

All these strategies of accepting the blame are nothing more than enabling. The longer you spend looking at yourself as the culprit, the less time you have to stop the real culprit, drug use. It is drugs that are destroying your child. That's the immediate problem. Sure, there may be a lot of negatives in the family— from a divorce, from working parents, anything. But the immediate concern is drug use and *how to stop it.* Blaming doesn't solve the problem. And the longer you are willing to accept the blame, the longer the druggie kid is free to continue using drugs. After all, you've given him a message that doing drugs is not his fault. It's yours. Or it's a certain event. A certain situation. Blaming is enabling.

So take yourself off the hook. It's not your fault. Then take the next important step and put your druggie kid ON the hook, where he belongs. He made the choice to do drugs. Blame him, not yourself.

Fixing It

The parent who makes up alibis for the cops, who writes excuses for the kid who skips school, who agrees to let the child who is burnt out or hung over stay home from school sick is fixing druggie behavior.

Cathy came home night after night vomiting her guts out. Every morning her mother would agree to let her stay home from school until she was over this "virus." Somehow, Cathy recovered miraculously every afternoon just in time to go out and get high with her friends. By midnight, she'd be vomiting her guts out again. By continuing to allow Cathy to stay home from school and sleep off the drugs, her mother enabled her to do more drugs. She rested all day and got high all night. And her mother only fixed it so that she could repeat the pattern over and over again. It was real easy to keep getting zonked with Mom's help.

There are three kinds of fixing: (1) Fixing the *situation,* such as parents who move to different schools, different neighborhoods, even different states to change the child's "bad environment." It's called the geographical fix. (2) Fixing the behavior, such as the parent who buys the child a horse, a dirt bike or a surfboard to steer the kid's interest toward more constructive behavior. They are trying to substitute new good behavior for bad drug-produced behavior. (3) Fixing the consequences, such as the parent who pays off the neighbor who was burglarized by the child or hires an expensive lawyer to get the kid out of a criminal charge.

Making a Treaty

A treaty is a two-sided agreement. It requires a negotiation of a trade-off between the participants—in this case, the parent and the child. This type of enabling occurs when one or both parents enter into a pact with the druggie kid that it is okay to do drugs because in some way the kid is *entitled.* For example, a learning or physical disability, or a bad experience with a drunken parent or grandparent or even a sibling who outshines the druggie kid may constitute a need for a pact. "Poor Johnny, he feels so bad, he deserves to have a little more freedom."

Sarah's parents made a treaty with her because she was overweight. Sarah was in and out of trouble at school. She was constantly fighting with her brothers and sisters. But her parents blamed it on low self-esteem. "If Sarah weren't overweight she wouldn't get into all this trouble." So the parents looked the other way while Sarah got seriously involved with drugs. The school problems and the family problems only got worse but the parents still thought they were fat problems. When summer rolled around, Sarah's parents decided the rest of the family could do without a summer vacation. Instead, they spent the $700 they had saved to go to the beach on a fat farm for Sarah. It would be worth it, they thought, if Sarah could lose weight and feel good about herself and then all her troubles would disappear. Instead, Sarah got high at the weight camp, stole a counselor's car and wrecked it. The treaty they agreed to enter into with Sarah only allowed her to continue using drugs with their "blessing."

It's Nothing New

The parent who looks at kids doing drugs and alcohol and compares it to his own experiences growing up is deceiving himself: The father who jokingly remembers the time he tried smoking, smoked a whole pack of cigarettes and got so sick he never did it again; or the father who recalls the time he and his friends bought a six-pack after a football game and couldn't remember going home. The pot and alcohol that kids use regularly in school today cannot be compared to the sneaking of a cigarette behind the gym that most parents remember from their schooldays.

Parents who write off their kids' drug use figuring that the kid will outgrow it are in for a rude awakening. And the parent who deceives himself into believing there's nothing new about kids doing a little experimenting is in for some bad news. If you think pot and alcohol are just two of the little things kids do growing up these days, then you're probably giving your own parents' seal of approval to doing drugs and alcohol. Not acknowledging the legitimate danger of drugs and alcohol and letting your child think you see drugs as part of the growing up experiment is enabling.

The recent attention in the mass media to marijuana and cocaine use has made drugs seem normal. That is as much the result of antidrug groups as it is of prodrug lobbyists. What has happened is that the consciousness level about drug use has been raised to such a point that people accept drug use as an inextricable part of American society—and particularly of adolescence.

It's Not So Bad

If you and your child have an agreement that marijuana is okay as long as he doesn't do drugs that are "harmful," you're enabling. Or if you agree with your child, "if you're going to do it, at least don't do it at school or out in the car where you can get arrested, do it at home where I can at least supervise it," you're enabling. The parent who enters into this kind of enabling is giving the biggest okay sign of them all.

Kids who agree to limits cannot keep their end of the bargain. The increasing tolerance of their bodies for the drugs combined with their weakening internal controls means that a kid will inevitably break his agreement. Then he's getting high at home with your blessing *and* away from home, with your blindness.

A mother recalled how she was afraid she was losing her closeness with her daughter. They had always had fun together, shopped together, worked in the house together and done projects together. When she felt her daughter slipping away, she was desperate to hang on to the relationship. So desperate that she agreed to try pot one day with her daughter. There they sat in the daughter's room smoking marijuana. Is it any wonder that the daughter told her friends how "cool" her mother was? This one incident stuck in the daughter's mind as her mother's seal of approval to do drugs. And the mother couldn't understand what happened when she ended up waiting in a hospital emergency room after her daughter had overdosed.

Letting your child smoke in his room, letting him have friends over to smoke or trying it yourself just to be a pal is blatant enabling, all giving the same message. "It's okay. Keep doing it."

The Protective Alliance

Sometimes parents band together with a child against other members of the family: the parent who says, "You're like me. We're both the quiet type. I understand you," or the parent who says, "I was always getting in trouble when I was your age, too. Your mother doesn't understand you but I do." That sort of fraternity is asking for trouble. The kid says to himself, "It's okay to do drugs because Mom will understand or Dad will understand. They said they were just like me when they were my age." The parent who is not in the fraternity, the parent who is trying to stop drug use and drug behavior becomes the enemy. This strategy creates a family situation that is divisive and enabling.

Wanting a Better Life

Most parents acknowledge that what they want most for their kids is a happy life. And what parents usually do in the name of a happy life is enabling. Parents give their children all the material possessions and opportunities that they never had themselves. Parents want their children to have a good time. They figure, "Life is hard enough as it is. It's a tough world kids grow up in today." Parents make adolescence a long play period for their children: "They're going to have hard times soon enough. Let them have fun while they can."

This way, parents end up contributing to a kid's drug use. They enable their children by smiling on the extended play period of adolescence. But drugs should have nothing to do with being a kid or having fun. And telling kids to have fun while they can, because the world is tough out there, is like giving them a license to do drugs. Adulthood, responsibility, hard times are just around the corner, so why not find all the highs they can now—that's the message parents are giving when they enable their kids to have a "happy life."

Drug use produces selfishness. The need to get high, the need to feel good, supersedes all other feelings and responsibilities in a druggie kid's life. When the child becomes self-centered, he begins to manipulate his parents and to be dishonest. The druggie kid encourages his parents to be enablers because it's in his own self-interest. The longer the parents enable, the more drugs he can do.

A druggie kid knows just when to lie, just when to throw a temper tantrum, just when to make you feel guilty about being too strict, just when to make you feel like you're old-fashioned and out of it, just when to tell you what you want to hear and just when to cry. As soon as those tears start to roll down the cheeks, parents melt. They trip over themselves trying to enable their child. "Poor baby, so she made a little mistake. Look how much she's hurting. She's learned her lesson. She'll never do it again." They clean up the mess, tell her what a good girl she is and how much they love her and will take care of her. And before the tears are dry, the child is thinking about getting high again.

Parents should learn from that kind of experience. Some do. The next time, the tears don't work quite so easily. The druggie kid knows it, so he adds some intense hugs to the bait. That works. Parents eat it up. Before they know it, they're enabling again. Fixing the behavior, supporting the kid and taking all the pain away.

But parents do get increasingly battleweary with each episode. So when the tears and hugs together don't work, the druggie kid turns to false promises. "I'll never do it again, Mom. I promise. I'm sorry I hurt you. I love you, Mom, I really do." What parent wouldn't buy that? It's the kind of stuff parents love to hear. It's the kind of stuff Walt Disney movies are made of. And sure enough, right on cue, the parent enables all over again.

The sad thing about all of this is that the more parents give, the more they help, the more druggie kids take advantage and the more they manipulate. We're back to the self-perpetuating cycle. Parents who are really and truly trying to help their children end up getting beaten over and over again by their kids. Kids not only don't appreciate the parents' efforts to help them, they eventually start to expect it and later even scoff at it: "You care so much about that school. You go straighten it out. I'm not going back there unless you get your ass over there and talk to those teachers, the bitches."

The dishonesty, selfishness and manipulation grow into out-and-out parent abuse. The more the parents try to love the druggie kids and take care of them, the more the kids put them down. And the parents are feeling more and more defeated. Like failures as parents. Like they've let their child down. Like there must be something they could have done to have prevented all this. Hurt. Angry. Unloved. And helpless.

And it all happened because they enabled their children. Because they loved their children and cared about them. Because they thought they were helping.

No matter how or why parents enable, it is dangerous. Not intervening when your kid brings home the friends you don't like is dangerous. Getting him out of trouble with the police is dangerous. "Understanding" because you were adventure-some as a child yourself is dangerous. Not banding together as parents, lying to each other to protect the child is dangerous. Talking the school into giving your child one more chance is dangerous. Doing drugs or alcohol yourself is not expecting your child to get the message, is past dangerous. It's criminal.

Whether you enable your child by your own chemical needs, leading him to believe that chemicals (drugs or alcohol) to make you feel good are okay . . . whether you enable your child by removing all the negative consequences of his drug-use . . . whether you enable out of loving and caring or ignorance and misunderstanding . . . it's still an engraved invitation to trouble. Don't load the gun and hand it to your child.

Parent Enabling Checklist

1. *Are you ignoring troubling behavior in your child? Are things changing in terms of his behavior, appearance, moods, and you're feeling uncomfortable, but it's not "bad enough" yet?*
2. *Are you making excuses for your child to your spouse, to teachers, or to other family members? Are you passing your child's behavior off as a learning problem, as being troubled with puberty, as an angry reaction to a divorce or some other physical or psychological problem?*
3. *Do you hide things from your spouse? Do you conspire with your child to keep the other parent from getting angry and laying down the law?*
4. *Have you accepted the fact that "all kids" do a little pot or alcohol? If so, have you tried to control it by agreeing to let your child smoke or drink only* at home?
5. *Are you unconvinced of the seriousness of the problem? Do you think maybe it's just the kid's form of social drinking?*
6. *Have you accepted the fact that all kids have to sow wild oats, and that includes drinking a little and smoking a little pot? Have you indicated approval by telling a few wild oats stories from your own youth?*
7. *Are you trying to control your child's use by permitting drinking, smoking, pot, paraphernalia or pot plants at home?*
8. *Do you have to have a drink or two at the end of the day to relax? Is alcohol a necessary part of each day for you and your spouse?*
9. *When you are skeptical about your child's behavior or excuses, do you press on for the truth or do you drop it because you are afraid of what you might find out? Do you hold your child accountable for his own actions or do you clean up the messes and protect him?*
10. *Have you gotten your child out of trouble at school or with the police?*

5

Societal Enabling
"Plop, plop, fizz, fizz."

American society is a society of media messages. Radio, television, movies, music, magazines, billboards all tell us that we should stay young, be sexy and feel good. It's the American way.

Teenagers have to assimilate all those messages and combine them with the bombardment of messages, demands, expectations, offers and orders they get at home. Grow up. Be responsible. Get smart. Go to college. Wash your face. Get a job. Clean up your room. Come home early. Get better grades. Get better friends. Work harder. Don't be a baby. Act like an adult. Quit acting like a kid. Don't act so grown up. Act your age. Is it any wonder kids are confused?

One day they're cute little toddlers. Then wham, their bodies grow up and suddenly they're supposed to be cool. They're supposed to play Pac-Man better than anybody else. They're supposed to wear the designer jeans that make them popular.

113

They're supposed to use the toothpaste that makes them sexy. They're supposed to drink the beer that athletes drink. And above all else, they're supposed to feel good all the time.

Kids are more reactive than active. They learn more from what they see than what they hear. They are told, "Don't drink." "Don't do drugs." But what they see is adults feeling good from alcohol and drugs. Adults drink to celebrate a success. They drink to compensate for a failing. They drink to your health. They drink to your happiness. They drink to the good life. Adults take pills to get rid of a headache, to dry up the sniffles, to make them skinny, to make them sleep, to wake them up. "Plop, plop, fizz, fizz. Oh, what a relief it is." Ours is a self-medicating society. And children imitate adults.

So, maybe you don't feel good all the time; but at least you shouldn't feel bad. Feeling bad is unnatural. When you go to the doctor, you're not so much looking to get well as you're looking to feel good. It's all right if the flu takes a few days to go away, just quick, Doc, give me something to make me feel better. I don't care if it's a pill or a shot as long as it makes me feel good fast.

Or like the man who comes stumbling home from the office in the television commercial. His tie is loose. His hat is on crooked. He's a mess. He's had a bad day at the office. He heads—where else?—to the medicine cabinet. Surely there's something in there to make him feel better.

Or the beer commercial that shows guys coming off the soccer field, off the construction site, off the tugboat. Suddenly, they walk through the door of a rustic bar and the sweat, the dirt, the furrowed brows all disappear. One beer turns them into smiling macho men.

Getting high is a sport. It's fun. That same picture that used to apply only to alcohol now applies to drugs too. There are plenty of adults who smoke a little pot with friends now and then or snort a little cocaine when their crazy friends come in from out of town. Marijuana and cocaine are no longer considered dangerous or violations of the law or contrary to social mores—they're recreational. John Lennon called marijuana "a harmless tickle."

So society's message to kids is simple: Feel good. Pain is unnatural. Do something to make bad feelings go away fast. Get high for the sport of it.

ALCOHOL: THE AMERICAN RITUAL

"GOD, COUNTRY AND APPLE BRANDY."

Alcohol is as much a part of the American picture as credit cards and billboards.

Alcohol is enshrined in nearly every major American ritual. Americans drink to celebrate the birth of a child, a graduation, a marriage, a new job, a promotion, a fortieth birthday, a twenty-fifth wedding anniversary, the birth of a grandchild and so on. There are kegs of beer for picnics. Mai tais for those tropical vacations. Bloody Marys for early morning gatherings. Wine for gourmet meals. And a little brandy for nightcaps.

Alcohol crosses all ethnic, racial, sexual and economic lines. Booze is just as much a mainstay of the union meeting as it is at the exclusive private club brunch. If you're having a good time, some sort of alcohol is a necessary ingredient to the mix.

But booze doesn't belong exclusively to the fun-loving. Alcohol is also seen as the remedy for drowning one's sorrows, the pain of an argument, the pain of divorce or the pain of death. And more trivial occasions deserve a drink too. What about the home team losing? The boss yelling all day? The kids driving you crazy? The project at work being behind? Just generally having a bad day at the office? A fight with the neighbors? Even a flat tire?

There's the notion that you're not having a good time unless you have just a few too many. Or you haven't really celebrated an event unless you get a little drunk.

Part of this is due to the way the media romanticize alcohol.

Everywhere you look, ads tell you that you will be more handsome, more beautiful, more loved, more popular, more sophisticated and happier if you have a drink in your hand.

The wine commercial on television that shows a couple sitting by a fireplace. He says, "I love you." She looks shy, warm, almost tearful. "What's the matter," he inquires, "didn't anyone ever tell you that before?" "Not the right one," she answers. The message? If you buy our wine, maybe you'll find Mr. Right.

Magazine advertisements for alcohol make drinking sound exclusive, alluring and luxurious. "Splash into summer with the sassy taste. Seagrams 7 and Coke, or gingerale, or 7-Up. When it comes to summer parties, they're the coolest things under the sun. So stir sensibly and make your party a splash." This one, believe it or not, is an ad for a baby gift: It shows a little bottle of whiskey with a big pink bow and a note that says, "It's a girl." What ever happened to receiving blankets?

Television beer commercials advertise their product with slogans like "Turn it loose," "It's time to relax," "If you've got the time, we've got the beer," "Put a little weekend in your week." "Go for the gusto," "This day was made for having fun" and "You only go around once in life." Simply translated: "Get high, have fun, you deserve it."

And what about the sexy lady who calls a man and invites him over for a glass of sherry? She says, "It's downright upright."

All of which makes Madison Avenue happy. They don't care whether you buy booze for a luau or a formal dinner party, whether you drink to be sociable or to get drunk. Just buy it. And drink it.

Children are romanced by all of this, too. They watch their television heroes drink. In the hit comedy series "Mash," Alan Alda and Mike Farrell brewed their own in their tent to cope with the stresses of war. The Ewing clan gathers in the living room weekly on "Dallas" to have a drink and a family squabble. People in the daytime soap operas meet in bars all the time. And off-camera, Johnny Carson, America's late-night king of comedy, got arrested for drunk driving.

Movie heroes drink. *Arthur* with Dudley Moore was one of the most successful pictures of 1981. It was about a drunk, a rich drunk, a comedy about a rich drunk. Everybody laughed. Paul Newman was nominated for an Academy Award in 1982 for playing an alcoholic lawyer in *The Verdict.* He lost the award but won the case. The 1983 movie *The Big Chill* is about a group of college buddies who got together for a weekend of drinking and smoking pot because one of their friends committed suicide. All of this adds up to a message that alcohol is a normal part of American life.

THE DRUG MESSAGE

"The new American ritual."

It wasn't so long ago that alcohol was social and drugs were taboo. Drugs were something that belonged in the slums or in the "art" community. And alcohol belonged in living rooms. Drugs meant people with needle marks up and down their arms. And drinks were something you invited people over for, like conversation. But now the twain have met.

There are as many songs today with references to drugs as to alcohol. As many jokes on television. As many scenes in movies.

Eric Clapton has a song called "Cocaine." The lyrics talk about using cocaine to help you when you're down and out.

A number of Beatles songs are believed to have made allusions to drugs. "Lucy in the Sky With Diamonds" is said to be a song about LSD (Lucy, Sky, Diamonds). The Beatles always denied the accusation, but kids consider it a druggie song.

Jefferson Airplane recorded a song called "White Rabbit" about pills that make you seem larger or smaller, like "Alice in Wonderland" [referring to the distortion one experiences on acid trips].

Or the Eagles' song called "Life in the Fast Lane" about

cocaine use. Or the very direct message of the Bob Dylan song, "Everybody Must Get Stoned."

It's impossible to listen to the "Top Thirty" rock list without being shocked at the actual number of references to drug use. Teenagers look up to rock stars, who ride around in Rolls-Royces and limousines, live in big houses and own private jets —the same people who do music about drugs and who get arrested for drug possession and drug use. To the adolescent, it looks like an enviable lifestyle. Rock stars are successful, they have money and power and they do lots of drugs. Many, in fact, say that drugs make them better musicians, better performers. When Paul McCartney was arrested for possession, he told newsmen he believed marijuana should be legalized.

To the rational person, those messages would be offset by the tragic deaths of rock stars like Janis Joplin, Jimi Hendrix, Jim Morrison of the Doors, Brian Jones of the Rolling Stones, punk rocker Sid Vicious of the Sex Pistols and comedy hero John Belushi. Kids should be able to look at the number of hero overdoses and put the two together. Not so. In fact, it is quite the opposite. Kids on drugs will tell you that those people "died cool." They were "feeling good, getting high."

Druggie kids don't look at drug deaths as tragedies. Example: "Janis Joplin did all sorts of drugs and her death was really famous. People still to this day worship her." "Bond Scott from the group A.C./D.C. died the way I wish I could." "It was cool the way Jim Morrison died." "I want to die the way Jimi Hendrix died. He died flying high."

Many kids view the ultimate high as the one that kills them. It is not unusual to listen to kids talk about the fantasy of their deaths on drugs, whether it be from an overdose or, as they say, "shooting the peace sign and running head-on into the car coming at them."

The musical message to "do drugs" comes at kids from records, T-shirts and radio stations. Stations that appeal to the adolescent market make open references to getting high. A Los Angeles radio rock station has a show they call "The Smoking

Hour" every day at five o'clock. What that says to kids is that's the way to end the day. If you're coming home from school or coming home from work, light up and take the weight off.

The "do drugs" messages do not stop here. Drugs have become an easy way for comedians to get laughs. The same uneasy laughs that comedians used to get by throwing the word "sex" around they now get with drugs. The Johnny Carson monologue at the beginning of "The Tonight Show" has regular references to the band's use of pot and coke. The audience always laughs, so the joke keeps getting recycled, like Ed McMahon drunk jokes.

Records and television aren't the only culprits. Woody Allen's movie *Annie Hall* won the Academy Award for best picture in 1977. In it, Diane Keaton smoked pot to reach a climax. And of course, every red-blooded American is entitled to an orgasm, even if it takes marijuana to get there.

Movie director Steven Speilberg has become a hero among adolescent moviegoers with films like *Jaws, Close Encounters of the Third Kind, E.T.* and *Poltergeist. Poltergeist* was rated PG and in it the parents get high. The children go to bed and Mom and Dad go off to their bedroom and smoke a joint. The kids loved it.

In the movie *Nine to Five,* Lily Tomlin, Jane Fonda and Dolly Parton get together after work and smoke pot. Just a few girls from the office having a good time.

The Cheech and Chong movie *Nice Dreams* is about guys who peddle drugs out of an ice cream truck. In the Burt Reynolds movie *Starting Over,* someone asks a group of people in a department store if anyone has a Valium—and everybody in the store responds by dipping into their private supply and handing over a pill.

The sex symbol of the eighties, Bo Derek, smoked pot in the movie *10.* Jamie Lee Curtis and her teenage companion, the daughter of a cop, are shown riding along getting high driving a car in John Carpenter's movie *Halloween.* That movie became a cult sensation among adolescents.

When sports heroes talk about drug use, kids see that as "He's a great ballplayer. Drugs must not be so bad for you. This guy's an athlete." Dodgers pitcher Steve Howe talked about how drug use hurt his personal life and almost destroyed his career. But kids don't hear that part. They only hear what they want to hear and that is: Sports figures make a lot of money, have a lot of fun and do drugs. Miami Dolphin all-pro running back Mercury Morris was sentenced to twenty years in prison for trafficking in cocaine. He sold $120,000 worth of coke to an undercover agent. To the druggie kid, he was an athlete, he was successful and he was cool.

Less blatant but equally convincing is the message to "do drugs" in the advertising of over-the-counter drugs. Everything from "How do you spell relief?" and of course, relief is a pill, to the ad for diet pills in which an attractive suburban housewife type says, "When I wanted to lose weight, I went to see my pharmacist." Not her doctor, not a nutritionist, not a fat farm, not an exercise class, HER PHARMACIST.

There's a pill which commercials call "the sleep aid for the eighties." It asks the probing question, "Do you have trouble sleeping at night because you take your job to bed with you?" Or the painkiller that tries to make people cope with the havoc in their lives, "When times got tougher, we got stronger." Or the ad for sleeping pills which lullabys "safe and restful, sleep, sleep, sleep." Madison Avenue would have you believe there's a pill for every problem, a capsule for every catastrophe. The message to kids is simple: "Drugs are a normal part of American life."

SHOPPING THE MESSAGE

"FOR SALE! DRUG SIGNS."

It is possible legally to buy drug paraphernalia in almost any city, small town or suburb in this country. You can buy rolling papers in the smallest country store. You can buy roach clips in record stores. You can buy pot pipes in head shops. You can buy incense in import shops and Oriental gift stores. And if all the stuff that goes with getting high is sold legally, then kids say, "So what's the big deal, they couldn't sell the pipes legally if marijuana were so bad for you."

In many cities, there are stores which go as far as selling pills. Caffeine pills and look-alike quaaludes can be sold legally, and ten-year-olds can walk up to the counter, plunk down their allowance and get higher than a kite. Paraphernalia shops and even some convenience stores sell little brown bottles labeled "Rush" or "Locker room" which contain amyl nitrate. Kids "huff" this substance—once used to treat heart patients—for a sixty-second high that has the sensation of thrust, like a rocket ship taking off. This drug is particularly dangerous for any child with the most minor heart variation, heart murmurs, etc. It can—and has—caused death.

Many young kids take on the druggie lifestyle long before they ever try drugs. They wear the marijuana leaf belt buckle they bought at the leather shop. They burn incense in their rooms when there's no drug smell to cover up. They buy T-shirts with messages about getting high or stoned. They listen to the druggie radio stations, buy the records and go to the concerts. Kids who act the part but don't do drugs are called "dry druggies," but they usually don't stay dry long. The lifestyle lures them in.

Any kid, any age, can walk through a shopping mall and within thirty minutes, be fully equipped for getting high. The bookstore in that same mall is likely to carry more books on how to grow marijuana and how to use drugs than on the hazards of drug use. There are several books on the market on how to turn your bathroom into a home laboratory to make synthetic drugs from chemicals found at the corner drugstore or in a school science class. And there are books cataloging commonplace plants, spices and chemicals which will produce a high.

For example, did you know that kids pick and eat morning glory seeds? They are a mild hallucinogen. Did you know that dried banana peels are a well-known way to get high? Kids take banana peels and dry them in the oven or microwave, crumble them and smoke them. The high they describe is "headaches and dizziness." Sounds like fun, doesn't it? From the spice cabinet, kids smoke poppy seeds, rosemary, oregano and bay leaves. They boil nutmeg in water and drink it for a mild high. They smoke dried tea leaves and get dizzy. From the medicine cabinet, kids spread toothpaste on cigarettes, let it dry and then smoke them. They claim it gives them a head rush. They drink large quantities of an over-the-counter sleeping aid called Nyquil because it contains alcohol. They sniff nail polish and nail polish remover for a brief rush. From the desk drawer, they get correction fluid and huff it. And from the garage, they get insecticides which they spray on dried parsley and smoke. All this information on how to get high with "things you have in your own home" is found in books sold at your local bookstore.

Twenty-four-hour convenience stores, the other place where druggie kids hang out, sell much of the apparatus. The Southland Corporation, which owns and operates 7-Eleven Stores all over the country, took a stand against drugs and removed rolling papers (papers used for making marijuana joints) from all of its company-operated stores. The decision was made by company president, Jere W. Thompson, the father of seven children, and it was the decision of a parent, not a businessman. The removal of the papers from the stores cost the company seven million dollars in annual profits—not sales, profits. SEVEN MILLION DOLLARS. The decision was made in 1979. To date, the loss of revenue totals thirty million dollars. But 7-Eleven has stuck by its decision.

Not many businesses have shown such social conscience. So kids of any age are free to buy as many bongs, roach clips, pot pipes and papers as their allowances will allow. And the message to them is simple: "Drug paraphernalia is a normal part of American life."

THE MEDIA DEBATE

"THE PROS-1. THE CONS-0."

Adolescents who read the newspaper or listen to the evening news might find it hard to figure out who's winning the marijuana debate. Because for every story about the research that shows the harmful effects of marijuana on the system, there's one about the lobby to legalize marijuana use. For every story about a child's death from drugs, there's a story about the use of marijuana for glaucoma victims and as an antinausea drug to treat the side effects of chemotherapy. Well, here are the facts: *marijuana is not used to treat glaucoma or nausea.* What *IS* used is a synthesized pill made of pure THC (one of over 400 chemical compounds found in marijuana). Marijuana is a dirty weed with many side effects, and the attempts to legislate marijuana cultivation and sale through pharmacies for "medical purposes" are deceptive, at best.

Those stories about the medical profession's use of marijuana and THC get passed along from druggie kid to druggie kid, who of course cite them as rationale for the drug use: "See Mom, it's good for you. Even doctors say so. It doesn't hurt you." Or the child who says, "You're living in the dark ages, Dad. They wouldn't be trying to legalize marijuana if it were so bad for you. In twenty years, everybody will be smoking grass. It'll be just like having a beer. You're so old-fashioned."

Cover stories about cocaine and marijuana in major news magazines make kids feel like they're part of the "in" crowd. They know what it's all about.

The eleven o'clock news comes on and the anchorman says, "Authorities say cocaine use is up twenty-five percent." Kids listen to that. The more people use drugs the more kids can justify their own use.

Researchers and drug-treatment people have maintained for ten years that the THC chemical found in marijuana is harmful to the respiratory equipment, the heart, the sexual organs and the brain. A University of California study says that one joint of marijuana produces many times the blockages in air passages and three times the precancerous lesions in the lungs as an entire pack of cigarettes. But kids don't hear those stories or cite those statistics. Instead they remember the stories of certain state assemblymen who, every year, introduce a bill to legalize marijuana use. So kids select the media message that says drug use is okay.

In several cities and states, possession of or use of marijuana has been reduced to a misdemeanor and a minimum fine. A kid using or possessing small amounts of marijuana is issued a citation that looks like a traffic ticket. He can mail in his fine without ever crossing the courthouse door. The media carry stories of these reduced offenses, leading kids to believe that marijuana use is no more against the law and the mores of society than jaywalking.

So the media message to kids is: "Some people think drugs aren't so bad for you. Sometimes they're even good for you." That's the way they hear it.

PRESCRIPTION DRUGS

"Need a high? Call a doctor."

People go to the doctor to feel better as much as they go to the doctor to get well. Consequently, doctors are used for passing out prescriptions and doling out drugs to make people feel good. It's a lot easier for the doctor to give a patient a "harmless" pill, a placebo to make him *think* he's feeling better, than it is to explain his psychological needs to him.

So there have evolved certain buzz words in the medical community. You say "pain," you get a prescription for Darvon or codeine. You say "can't sleep," you get a prescription for Valium or another tranquilizer. You say "nervous," you get a prescription for lithium.

Kids know the buzz words. Listen to these kids' accounts of how they conned doctors out of medicine to get high.

DAVE: "I told the doctor I always felt nervous and jittery. He asked me if I had had hypertension previously. I told him I had and he wrote me a prescription for Ritalin."

PAUL: "I had broken my leg and long after it healed I kept complaining about how much it hurt. The doctor told me to take aspirin at first. I told him that the aspirin didn't help and I couldn't stand the pain. He gave me codeine."

CAROLYN: "I went to see a psychiatrist and he asked me a lot of questions about school. I told him I couldn't sleep at night . . . that I just would lie in bed awake all night . . . so the next day at school I couldn't concentrate. He diagnosed me as a manic depressive and gave me a prescription for sleeping pills."

SUE: "I had been sick with a cold and I told the doctor the drug I wanted. I told him I wanted Drixorol. He gave me the prescription but then I called him and told him that I spilled them and they got wet and ruined. So I asked for some Benadryl. And he gave it to me."

LORI: "These are all separate occasions that happened with the same psychiatrist. First I told him I was nervous all the time and couldn't calm down. He prescribed lithium. Then I complained of more nerve problems. He gave me Thorazine. Then I claimed I was having problems sleeping. He gave me Placidyl. Finally, I told him I was having convulsions from nerves. He gave me Tegretol and later Haldol and Dilantin."

TOM: "I had dental surgery but after it was all over I would pick at my gums before I would go into the dentist for the checkup so I could tell him how much my gums hurt and get codeine."

TROY: "I went to the doctor for asthma. I told him I was having a hard time breathing, that it hurt. He examined me and said, 'Does it hurt here?' I told him it hurt but it really didn't. He gave me a shot of adrenalin and a prescription for morphine and Theo-Dur." Even kids being treated for drug use know what to say to get the drug they want.

SHERYL: "I was in the hospital for drugs and I would throw tantrums so they would give me something to calm me down."

CURT: "I was in a drug rehabilitation program and I told the doctor I couldn't sleep so he would give me sedatives."

KAREN: "I was in a drug rehabilitation center. I told them I was happy one minute and depressed the next. They gave me lithium, big bottles of it."

When doctors freely hand out pills, they are handing out a philosophy too . . . the philosophy that feeling good is normal, feeling bad is abnormal. The unconscious message to kids? "Some drugs are okay."

MENTAL DRUGS
"GIVE YOUR CHILD THE FREEDOM TO GROW UP."

Some of the people most guilty of Societal Enabling are the counselors, psychiatrists and psychologists who say that pot smoking is normal, that kids who try a little marijuana or drink a little are just experimenting with growing up. This kind of "professional" advice encourages parents to look the other way. It gives them a good excuse to practice Parent Denial.

Those same professionals are the ones who enable by advocating fewer rules and more room for the kid to spread his adolescent wings. With drugs, kids do not translate fewer rules as responsibility—to them it means a chance to do drugs and feel good without consequences. It is not a chance parents can afford to take.

This is what happens: A parent gets concerned with the problems the kid is getting into and goes to a counselor to get help. The kid cons the counselor, just like he's conned his parents, by complaining about the family. The kid maintains that his bad behavior is just a reaction to everything that is wrong at home, when the real reason for the out-of-control family is the kid's drug use. The counselor's advice? "You're really restricting the child too much. That's why there is so much friction. Try getting along without so many rules." No rules give the kid more space to hide his drug use and the problems only get worse.

Therapists are not the ones who sit up all night waiting for a child to come home. They are not the ones who get the rash of phone calls from the school. They are not the ones who live with the irrational behavior at home. They are not the ones who have to go to the emergency rooms when the child overdoses. They are not the ones who have to get the knock on the door from the police at two o'clock in the morning. So the therapist who tells parents they are holding the reins too tight on a child using drugs is asking for trouble for the drug-torn family.

Counselors in the mental health field also enable druggie kids when they encourage parents to befriend their children. Children don't need friends. They need parents. They need someone to turn to for limits. The "be a pal" school of parenting is like asking a child to make good grades without the benefit of teachers and books. *When psychologists, psychiatrists or any mental health counselors deal with children, it has to be made clear that drug use IS THE problem, not the result of a problem.* School problems and family problems cannot be dealt with unless the drug use stops. School problems don't cause a kid to take drugs. Family problems don't cause a kid to take drugs. Drugs are the problem. Pure and simple.

But parents are disarmed by degrees. They assume anybody with an M.A., an M.D. or a Ph.D. must know what he's talking about. Americans have magical beliefs in the competence of the professional and scientific communities. This guy went to school six or eight years to tell you how to make your family work. He must be right.

Not necessarily.

The counselor who says "trying drugs is normal" or "drug-use is symptomatic" or "something else is wrong in the child's life" is an enabler. And the counselor usually ends up throwing in the towel on the kid, leaving the parents with a bigger problem than they had to begin with. Be selective when you seek professional help; there are many people in the mental health field who are not enablers.

To a kid, the "it's normal" message translates as "it's part of growing up, it's okay." The "drugs are a symptom" message translates as "if my parents were right, if school were different, I wouldn't smoke dope." All of which adds up to a mental health message: "It's not your fault. It's really okay to keep using."

ACADEMIC ENABLERS
"DEALING WITH THE SCHOOL DAZE."

Kids buy and use most of their drugs in public schools. And the response of school officials carries a message to kids about where adults stand on the drug issue. The teacher who knows a kid is stoned and does nothing about it is giving a message to a child that "adults aren't going to impose any consequences if you do drugs."

The teacher who wants to be "in" with the kids, wants to be accepted and thought of as being cool, is an enabler. If he or she says to a kid, "Looks like you had a tough night," and laughs, the teacher is enabling the kid by implying that drugs are fun.

Teachers who know kids are high in class and just try to keep them quiet so they don't disrupt the rest of the students are enablers. The teacher who says, "Just put your head down on your desk" when he knows the child is high or coming down or burnt out is giving a message that drugs are okay and adults will be sympathetic toward their use.

The school principal who finds out a child has missed several days, even weeks, of school and does not contact the family is an enabler.

The teacher who says, "If you're going to do drugs, just don't do them in my classroom," is an enabler. Does that mean that it's okay to do drugs other places at school? Or the teacher who says, "If you're going to do drugs, just don't do them at school." Does that mean that drugs are okay, as long as they're not at school? They should be for weekend use only?

And there are even more blatant types of enabling in the schools. Many students tell stories of buying drugs from teachers, selling drugs to teachers and even getting high with teachers. These teachers are obviously not only enabling by condoning but are *encouraging* drug use. And some kids have teachers who are role models for drug use.

MIKE: "One of my teachers used to put alcohol in her coffee cup and sip on it all day."

CRAIG: "I found a bottle in my math teacher's desk."

LINDA: "My physical education teacher used to tell us girls how he would get drunk and go out on his wife."

The school system itself is sometimes guilty of enabling. Take the fifteen-year-old boy who was trying drugs and getting into trouble at school. The problems persisted until the school put the child in an after-school program. What that meant was that the boy didn't have to be in class until 1:00 P.M. Supposedly, the smaller classes were meant to insure a more restricted environment and more discipline. Instead, it left the boy free all morning to get high while his parents were at work.

A girl who scored well on academic aptitude tests was having grade problems. She had never really lived up to her potential and had never been a great student but suddenly, because of her drug use, she was barely showing up for class. The final blow came when she sat through a test staring into space and only turned her paper over once to write her name on it. The school suggested to the parents that they consider a special classroom situation designed to help students with low motivation. The parents agreed. The girl was put in classes with other kids who didn't care, which gave very little homework and she only had to go to class four hours a day. Needless to say, she used drugs to fill the other hours.

The most common example of Societal Enabling at school is the teacher who ignores drug use and drug behavior simply because he is battleweary. In the past few decades, the teaching profession has deteriorated from the once highly respected position that it occupied in the community to an exhausting low-income job with few rewards. Low achievement, school violence, attitudes about integration and drugs have all culminated in a generation of teachers who feel too tired to do anything about drugs. There are too many kids doing it, too many parents who aren't willing to face the problem, too many frightened school administrators who don't even want to hear about it. One teacher remarked, "I got out of school really excited about teaching. Now I hate to go into class. Half the kids do drugs and they interfere with the rest of the kids who really want to learn." Another teacher said, "In the beginning I tried to do something about it. I was really scared for kids who were bright and able and started to fail in front of my eyes. The principal called me into his office and told me to stop sending kids to the dean's office—it was causing problems. The parents I called in to talk about their child's drug problem accused me of lying and made complaints about me to the school board. I'd really like to do something but I don't know what to do."

Schools ought to be a safe zone where kids can learn and where they can't get dope and get high. They aren't. Every time a child buys or sells drugs at school or gets high and nothing is done about it, the message to kids is loud and clear: "Yeah, the people in school don't do anything about it. It's okay."

CIVIL SERVANTS

"THE UNCIVIL MESSAGE."

Many kids on drugs tell stories of how a police officer stopped them and took their drugs away. In most cases, the police officer takes those drugs to the police station and the drugs are destroyed. But almost without exception, druggie kids believe that the cop kept the drugs and used them himself.

The police officer should have arrested the kid. The arrest would have stuck with him a lot longer than the lecture the officer gave. But because there are so many kids using drugs, because of the mind-boggling paperwork involved in the arrest and, to a large extent, because of the resistant attitude of most parents, officers often choose not to make an arrest for possession or use of marijuana. It's become one of those offenses where officers look the other way. They have given up. The courts don't impose penalties, the schools don't, the parents don't. So why should they?

Often in accident or traffic violation reports, when an adolescent has been using drugs, officers will write down alcohol use on the report, because alcohol use is much easier to determine than drug use. So, once again, the drug use gets passed by. No warning to parents. No consequences for the kid. As a result, he walks away believing that the police officer has kept the drugs, thus "cops do drugs too," and that drugs are "kinda against the law but nobody takes it seriously."

SOCIETAL ENABLERS

"The kids' view."

Listen to what these kids had to say about the Societal Enablers they dealt with daily.

KATY: "The lady down the street paid me with pot for watching her house."

KATHY: "The lady I babysat for kept a supply of pot, Quaaludes and speed."

MONA: "There was the fire chief that I knew and respected a lot. He had been a friend of my family's for a long time. But when my friend got high and set her parents' house on fire, he didn't mention drugs on the report."

SUE: "I went to a mental health center and they said that a little bit of pot and alcohol wouldn't hurt me."

CHERYL: "When I went to private school, I did drugs with my teachers."

KAREN: "I was high on pot and Quaaludes when I went to see my counselor and he didn't even know."

ANN: "When I was prostituting to get drugs, a lot of respectable businessmen would pick me up. Doctors would even pay me off with drugs."

TRACY: "I was over at this deacon's house from my church and he had a bunch of ups and downs."

TONY: "In seventh grade, I did ups and downs with the P.E. coach and he said it made him better at sports."

MIKE: "My counselor told me it was okay to do pot and alcohol as long as I didn't do anything heavier."

MARK: "I thought about how Cheech and Chong would go on stage and do drugs and get paid for it. I thought it was really cool."

PHIL: "I went to a lawyer who told me how to keep away from the cops and what kinds of rights I had with drugs, what kind of search procedures were allowed."

JEFF: "My girlfriend's father was a doctor and her mother was a nurse. We all did drugs together, pot, hash, ups and downs and different prescription drugs."

MICKEY: "My friend's uncle was a cop. And he told us just not to do drugs in public."

NANCY: "My grandfather was dying with cancer and they gave him pot."

KEN: "I went to a concert and kids were using drugs right in front of the police and the police did nothing about it."

JIM: "Keith Richard [from the Rolling Stones] got arrested for drugs a couple of times and I thought it was cool that he could get arrested and not go to jail."

NAN: "I got high with a Jesuit priest at my school."

Societal Enabling Checklist

1. Do you use patent or prescription medication to diet, to gain weight, to sleep, to stay awake or to relax?
2. Does your family find drug humor entertaining?
3. Do you let your child own and listen to records or tapes of prodrug, satanic, or hard or acid rock? Do you let him listen to them alone in his room?
4. Does he listen regularly to local hard-rock, prodrug radio stations? Does he plaster his wall with hard-rock idols or drug posters?
5. Do you let your child go to a lot of rock concerts or prodrug movies?
6. Do your local malls and stores sell drug-related paraphernalia? Have you wondered why they do, who buys and uses it? Have you seen any of it in your child's room?
7. Does your local bookstore have more books on how to use drugs than on the problems of drug use?
8. Will your family doctor prescribe you pain or mood-altering medication for minor illnesses? Do you allow your child to go to the doctor alone?
9. Do the teachers and principals and counselors in your school system deny or overlook drug problems? Do they call you if your child is absent to see if he's home sick?
10. Does your local police department arrest most or all kids found to be in possession? Does your justice system actively prosecute and routinely commit for treatment kids arrested for drug problems? What is your police department's record on arresting drug dealers?

6

Parent Action
"How to wage the war."

If you don't like the kids your teenager is bringing home anymore, if you can't talk to him over his hard-rock music anymore, if your teenager is short-tempered, moody, sleepy and quarrelsome, if your son or daughter ignores all household rules, then you better get out of that armchair and hit the ground running. Because your own home may be the battleground for the war against drugs.

The most important part of your strategy? *Know the Enemy.*

Learn everything you can about drugs: their names, their use, their effects on the body. Know the paraphernalia associated with drugs, learn to recognize it and how it is used.

And know your preparedness for battle. Assess your strengths and weaknesses. Know that the most important weapons you have are love and strength. You can't win the war without them—and without knowing how to use them.

"Before my son's group started experimenting with pot, I

didn't know drugs existed but now I've been to some parents' awareness programs and I know what is going on. My son has to work really hard to get around me.

"Information makes all the difference. Now I know what to look for and how to help my child."

THE ENEMY

"DRUGS, DRUGS AND MORE DRUGS."

For most people inexperienced in the drug world, drugs are marijuana, LSD, heroin and cocaine. Marijuana (pot) we learned about from the hippie movement. LSD came along with Timothy Leary and the "turn on, tune in, drop out" philosophy. Heroin is what we think people die from in Harlem. And cocaine is the expensive, elite drug of the fast-paced entertainment world.

If you've read this book carefully, by now you know the truth: Kids today get high on everything from cough syrup to whipped cream cans. Cough syrup? There's codeine in it. Whipped cream? It's the gas left in the can, which they inhale by holding the can's nozzle open and catching the gas in a paper bag. The same goes for deodorant cans, paint cans or any other type of aerosol can.

If you're like most parents you don't even understand what "getting high" feels like—but if you do make an association, it's probably with the "buzz" you get from alcohol. And, of course, the headache, bloodshot eyes, and queasy stomach of the morning after.

Well, all that barely scratches the surface.

"I would feel this sort of rush in my head. And I would feel real paranoid the whole time I was high. My body would feel real numb and tingly when I would touch other objects. Sometimes it felt like I was looking at everything through really foggy glasses. The first time I tried PCP I was thirteen, and I remember my whole body felt spongy. When I walked, I felt like I was walking on a huge lake. My ears were ringing, and I felt like my insides were going to blow up."

"I remember when I took speed, everything would get really fuzzy and blurry. It felt like I was dreaming. Like when I went swimming, I thought I was dreaming I was swimming. Then I thought I was swimming with sharks and I got really scared. I felt like I was dreaming because no matter what I did, I felt like I didn't really do it."

"Sometimes I felt like I was real tall. Then sometimes I would feel like I was really skinny. I would be standing up and I'd say things like, 'I can't stand up.' "

"I would just stare into space in a frozen position. It would be euphoric for a while but then I would start to feel paranoid and apathetic. I would buy Primatene, those over-the-counter tablets for asthma and take three or four of them. Then I'd get real nervous and shaky. Sometimes I would take Valium and Percodan together and it made me feel like I was going to throw up. My body felt like it was in turmoil. When I took acid, I lost all interest in things around me. I remember not being able to see things in their proper size. And I could hear noises like slow drums."

"At times I would want to reach for a cigarette or something and I couldn't control the movement of my hand or arm. I was fascinated by the fact that I had lost control and would often just sit back and think about myself out of control in relationship to the world around me. I would hear a lot of strange noises. Sometimes I thought a nun was whispering words in my ear I couldn't understand. I could hear bells ringing in the distance. Sometimes I would listen to music and just stare at something and fantasize that my body could expand and contract with the music. I felt relaxed and slowed down, minutes seemed like hours. I would confuse what my eyes saw with what my ears heard. While I was doing drugs, I felt distant, walled off from the rest of the world."

"When I was on pot, I would panic. I felt like I wanted to pull my hair out and scream. I felt like my whole body was being sucked through twisted, curly pipes. I felt like I was being banged against the walls and my brain was rattling inside my head. When I was on alcohol, I got to the point I was walking and throwing up at the same time. I was pissed off and ashamed of myself."

"I remember not being able to stay in one place for a minute. I would start breathing real fast and it felt like I was having a thousand thoughts at once. I was never satisfied where I was, if I was sitting in a chair or lying in bed. I couldn't get comfortable no matter what I did."

"I remember staring at my arm or my leg for hours at a time and wondering what their purpose really was. One time, I just stared in a mirror for hours, and the whole time I thought I was in the process of dying."

"I couldn't eat because food looked gross and distorted. I had chills and a big knot in my throat. I will never forget that pit feeling inside, just an eternal emptiness. I would have given anything to stop the effects of the drug. I literally hated the feelings. I was very, very uncomfortable and self-conscious. While I was on drugs, I wouldn't think I was worth shit. I would feel regret for the way I treated my parents, and I would get overwhelming guilt."

"I would see trails of light behind moving objects."

"I could remember parts of my day, but I couldn't feel my body. If I could eat, it felt like it took ten minutes for the tiniest piece of food to go down my throat. I was always afraid I was going to choke to death."

"I would mix quaaludes and beer and I would feel very tired and numb. I would mix them to get a better high. Sometimes I would pass out when I mixed them. I did two kinds of quaaludes. The boot-legged ones had one "m" in the word lemon that was printed on them. The prescription ones had two "m's" in lemon. I would smoke them in pot or cut them in two and put them up my nose."

"When I took PCP and started to get high, my lungs would feel sticky. I felt like I was trapped inside, like I was floating in the room, and I only wanted to be half that high. I didn't like feeling totally out of control. I wished that I could die to make the pain go away. When I looked in the mirror, I thought my face was pale white with black rings on it—like a vampire."

"I remember my lungs stinging and feeling like my body was going to explode."

"Sounds seemed very vivid. That's why I like sound effect music. I had a hard time understanding speech patterns because words would blend together."

"I felt like I had rubber legs."

"I would do things like stare at a statue and think it was the statue of death. And then I'd dance around it."

"Objects like cars would get bigger, then smaller, when I was high."

"My scalp tingled."

"I thought I was floating on earth, on the very edge looking out."

"I saw red and green stripes flash through the air."

"I thought acid let me use other parts of my brain normal people couldn't use."

"Sometimes I felt like my eyeballs might fall out."

"I had pains in my groin and I thought I was going sterile."

"My heart would beat really fast and I was afraid I might have a heart attack and die. It was really scary. But when the high went away, I'd just do it again."

"I did PCP and I remember getting enraged at the wall. I felt like I was watching myself hit the wall."

"I felt like my mind was separating from my body."

"I was in gym class once and I thought the floor was waving like the ocean. I thought the tiles were cracking, and the walls were falling apart."

A fourteen-year-old girl recalled her first acid trip: "I was anxious and scared because everybody said it was good. I took it. I felt like laughing. Things seemed okay. I thought it was fun, at first. Then my body started to shake out of control. I was in the woods and seeing double. I wanted the feeling to stop. I tried throwing up but I couldn't. I couldn't even hold still. My friends told me to take another hit, a purple microdot, that it would calm me down. I did it but all I wanted to do was cry. My brother and his friend kept telling me to think of nice things. I hated it. It wasn't what people told me it would be like. I slept for the next two days after I did it because I was so worn out. A couple of weeks later, I was doing it again."

Kids talking about being high. It doesn't sound appealing at all, does it? And kids themselves will sometimes say that getting high isn't always a good feeling. But they do it anyway.

There are four basic types of drugs:

Stimulants

Stimulants speed up the action in the pleasure center of the brain. Street stimulants include caffeine pills, amphetamines and cocaine, and are referred to by kids as "uppers." The chemical action of the stimulant increases the blood pressure and pulse rate, bringing the body to a higher level activity, eliciting feelings of exhilaration.

Depressants

Depressants, "downers," slow down the chemical action of the brain and the nervous system. Depressants include alcohol, barbiturates, tranquilizers and volatile solvents.

Disassociatives

These drugs disturb the information-processing functions of the brain. The user may think he's hearing things he sees or seeing things he hears. It's like the body has gotten all its wires crossed. Past memories may become confused with current perceptions. The equilibrium may be affected. Images may appear unreal or distorted. Disassociatives are also called hallucinogens. They include marijuana, LSD, mescaline and PCP (angel dust).

Narcotics

Narcotics are what the layman would call painkillers—drugs like morphine and codeine. But painkiller is a misnomer. Narcotics don't really kill pain, they just *interfere with the experience of pain.* In other words, it still hurts, you just don't care because the pain isn't registering in the brain. Narcotics are also called opiates and include opium, codeine, morphine, heroin and methadone. Percodan is one of today's most popular "white-collar" narcotics.

There may be some drugs in your child's room right now. The first step is knowing what they look like. A good place to look for help is a parents' group in your community. Local schools, the police department or social agencies have lists of such groups. Panda, Pac, Dream, Families in Action, Informed Parents are only a few of the organizations whose aim is to inform and help individual families and then to reach out into the community to help stop drug abuse.

These groups can help you recognize drugs and drug symptoms as well as the paraphernalia associated with drug use—spoons, roach clips (roach is the term for a partially smoked marijuana joint), syringes, droppers, needles, bongs, paper bindles, razors and tooters (a device for snorting cocaine).

As a parent, you owe it to yourself and to your children to learn about drugs and the drug culture. Determine the influences in your child's life: his friends, his hangouts, his school activities. The first time a child starts to pull away from the family and get close to his peer group is the time to assess the situation and take action. Remember: Know the Enemy.

	DRUG NAME	OFTEN PRESCRIBED BRAND NAME
1. Stimulants *(Ups)*	STIMULANTS Cocaine Amphetamines Others	(None) Benzedrine, Dexedrine Sanorex Voranil Pre-Sate
2. Depressants *(Downs)*	Alcohol	All advertised brand names.
	INHALANTS	Gasoline, lighter-fluid, aerosol cans. One of these is inhaled for about five minutes through a saturated cloth or in a bag covering the nose and mouth. This procedure is repeated as long as the child wants to remain high.
	OTHER DEPRESSANTS Chloral Hydrate Barbiturates Tranquilizers Methaqualone	Noctec, Somnos Nembutal, Seconal Valium, Miltown Quaalude
3. Disassociatives *(Hallucinogens)*	CANNABIS Pot Hash Hash Oil THC Marijuana	(None) Slang names: Pot, grass, joint, reefer.

POSSIBLE EFFECTS	OVERDOSE EFFECTS	HOW TO SPOT AN ABUSER
Increased alertness, excitation, dilated pupils, increased pulse rate and blood pressure, insomnia, loss of appetite.	Agitation, hallucinations, convulsions, possible death.	An almost abnormal cheerfulness and unusual increase in activity, jumpiness and irritability; hallucinations and paranoid tendencies after intravenous use.
Acts as a depressant. Dehydration, hyperactivity, nausea, headache, heartburn, thirst, giddiness.	Insomnia, delirium, hallucinations, convulsions, loss of memory.	Puffiness of the face, redness of eyes, depressed, disoriented.
Very alert, keen senses; possible hallucinations and dizziness, tightness in chest area.	Brain damage occurs when used over a long period of time. Hands become dry, chapped and may peel. Possible death.	Smells like whatever the child was huffing. Slow mental and physical response to conversation. Scrambled words and disconnected sentences.
Slurred speech, disorientation, drunken behavior.	Shallow respiration, cold & clammy skin, dilated pupils, weak and rapid pulse, coma, possible death.	The appearance of drunkenness with no odor of alcohol characterizes heavy dose. Sedation with variable ataxia.
Euphoria, relaxed inhibitions, disoriented behavior.	Fatigue, paranoia, possible psychosis.	Abusers may feel exhilarated or relaxed, stare off into space; be hilarious without apparent cause; have exaggerated sense of ability.

	DRUG NAME	OFTEN PRESCRIBED BRAND NAME
	HALLUCINOGENS	
	LSD	(None)
	PCP	(None)
	Mescaline	Semylan
	Peyote	(None)
	Mushrooms (Psilocybin)	Mushrooms, with a purple ring on stem close to collar, are picked out of cow dung. They may be eaten raw or boiled into a tea.
4. NARCOTICS *(Painkillers)*	NARCOTICS	
	Opium	(None)
	Morphine	Morphine
	Heroin	(None)
	Others	Dilaudid
		Paregoric
		Percodan

THE PLAN OF ATTACK

"THE BEST OFFENSE IS A GOOD DEFENSE."

The best kind of Parent Action has to do with the way you live your life every day—not *after* a family is being torn apart by drugs. It has to do with your marriage, how you see yourself in your family and how your children see themselves.

Sending for ammunition after you've already been fired upon doesn't exactly make for a strong defense.

Unfortunately, for most families, by the time you realize that your child is using drugs, you're already playing catch-up. The score is Drugs–1, Parents–0, and it's probably too late

POSSIBLE EFFECTS	OVERDOSE EFFECTS	HOW TO SPOT AN ABUSER
Illusions and hallucinations, poor perception of time and distance.	Longer, more intense "trip" episodes, psychosis, possible death.	Abusers may undergo complete personality changes, "see" smells, "hear" colors. They may try to fly or brush imaginary insects from their bodies, etc. Behavior is irrational. Marked depersonalization.
Cold sweats accompanied by hallucinations.	Stomach cramps, nausea and blackouts.	Beady eyes, nervous, uptight, erratic behavior, sweaty, laughing and crying.
Euphoria. Drowsiness, respiratory depression, constricted pupils, nausea.	Slow and shallow breathing, clammy skin, convulsions, coma, possible death.	Constricted pupils. Calm, inattentive, "on the nod," with slow pulse and respiration.

for you to fight the battle alone.

The first thing you have to do is make two major decisions: *(1) I am willing to change my own relationship with alcohol and drugs because of my concern for my child,* and *(2) I am willing to take charge.*

THE BATTLE CRY

"THIS FAMILY IS AN ANTIDRUG FAMILY."

It may seem self-evident that the family should take a firm, unwavering stand on ingesting mood-altering chemicals of any kind. But not every family does. Ask yourself these questions: Does your family ever laugh about someone who got really drunk, drunk enough to endanger himself or others? Have you accepted "trying drugs" as something all kids do these days? If so, you may very well be in trouble.

A healthy family's lifestyle absolutely must include good nutrition, good exercise and a positive attitude. A healthy family's idea of having fun and practicing good living absolutely must exclude chemically induced highs in favor of the natural highs that come from happy, fulfilling relationships and realistic, inspiring goals.

Every family must take a good look at its alcohol use pattern. Does dad have a drink as soon as he gets home from work? Is alcohol served daily in the home? Do you have to have booze to have fun at your house? Do Mom or Dad use alcohol when they've had a bad day? Does either become intoxicated when they drink?

The key word with alcohol use is moderation. Social use of alcohol as a beverage or with food is okay—but using alcohol as a tranquilizer, a disinhibitor or an intoxicator—numbing painful feelings—is *not* okay.

Younger families may also need to consider their use of drugs. The sixties generation has children who are old enough to be involved in drugs now. If kids see their parents use or talk about drugs regularly, they'll think, "They do it. It must be okay."

The family also needs to examine its attitude about self-medication. Take a look at the medicine cabinet. Do you see lots of outdated prescription drugs that nobody needs anymore? Are there over-the-counter medications for every possible pain, creak or ailment? Do the adults in your house have an attitude of "feel-a-pain, pop-a-pill"? Is anybody in the house regularly using painkillers of some description, anything from aspirin to morphine to medications with codeine? Does anybody in the house use tranquilizers on a regular basis? Or amphetamines for reducing? It's pretty hard to tell a kid not to use drugs to numb his own feelings during adolescence, if the adults are doing it for their problems.

The family medicine chest should contain aspirin or Tylenol, Band-aids, vitamins, a thermometer and any prescription currently used by a family member. Nothing more. If there are any prescriptions not in use, throw them out. If there is a legitimate reason for a painkiller (if you or your spouse has arthritis, for example), keep it locked up, out of the sight and reach of children and teenagers.

There are six basic rules for the drug-free family:

(1) no illegal drug use by anyone, (2) no misuse of prescription or patented drugs, (3) no alcohol use by minority-age kids in the family, (4) no routine alcohol use by adults—that is, no use pattern that communicates drinking as a necessary daily function, (5) no intoxication by adults and (6) no use of drugs to lose weight, gain weight, go to sleep, wake up or relax.

The real game here is for the whole family to take a new approach to handling the high and low spots of life. It is not enough to simply stop whatever negative practices with drugs and alcohol exist. Together, you must develop constructive ways to make life worthwhile.

WHO'S IN CHARGE?

"WOULD THE ADULT HERE PLEASE STEP FORWARD?"

The next step in a good family action plan is to find out who is really in charge.

In recent years, we have gone through a period of "disco parenting"—a school of psychology that proposes that parents should be buddies to their children.

Particularly if you're dealing with an adolescent drug user, you cannot afford to blur the distinction between the roles of the adult and the child. Kids need to grow up with the security of knowing that a caring, loving adult is *in charge.* They will never learn to be responsible adults if they have to learn to fly without a net, and parents are that net. And when children reach adolescence temptations are greater, problems more confusing. They need backup more than ever.

Being a parent is a *hard* job. And while you are never relieved of the responsibility of being a parent, the nature of parenting does change dramatically as the child grows. First, it changes when the child leaves the womb and is no longer physically dependent on the mother's body for life. It changes again when the child enters adolescence and starts to move out of the social, emotional, economic and spiritual orbit of the family. It changes again when the child finishes the adolescent passage and becomes an adult and leaves the immediate nuclear family to be part of a large extended family.

Parents don't always understand the stages of that separation. Many parents get the idea that adolescence is where freedom begins. But, as we've shown, freedom is not the answer for adolescents.

Twelve may be old enough to stay home and take care of a younger brother. Or old enough to go to the store alone. Or old enough to get a training bra. But it's not old enough for autonomy. Growing up means enlarging your arena. But the decision of when and how much to enlarge the arena should not be a kid's alone. As he demonstrates effectiveness in a safe arena, the parent may open the way to a slightly less safe, slightly larger arena. When that arena is safe, the arena is widened again. That's the way the adolescent passage should work.

To be an adult means to have self-esteem, a sexual identity, a sense of self-worth, goals and the tools with which to attain them. It means having the ability to cope with the wide variation of the human experience and the feelings that go along with it. The process of acquiring these qualities, traits and skills is a slow one and it requires adult supervision. So parents have to be parents and they have to let kids be kids.

Another part of the new parenting philosophy suggests that parents need to learn to compromise with their children. There are NO COMPROMISES where children and drugs are concerned. Parents are the ones who should make the decision about the safety and well-being of their children. Parents must acknowledge the availability and widespread use of drugs and let the children know how they feel about it. True, they should listen to the needs of adolescents, but if a kid says, "I won't do hard drugs if you'll let me smoke pot in my room," NO DEAL. Or, "I won't smoke pot if you will let me drink," NO DEAL. Or, "If you let me stay home from school today, I'll mow the lawn," NO DEAL.

The effect of no compromise is especially important in the case of divorced parents, where druggie kids will often play one parent against the other. But parents MUST present a unified front, whether living under the same roof or not. The child needs to know that *both* parents love him and will take responsibility for his safety and well-being.

Single parents are also prone to compromise out of guilt. If one parent is deceased or has no contact with the child, the remaining parent, feeling sorry for the child, may be weakened to a compromising position. The single parent, too, is looking for acceptance from the child since there is no other adult around to supply positive reinforcement.

A family has to operate on bottom-line values, and the parent has to be the keeper, teacher and enforcer of those values. The parents must decide what is acceptable behavior for family members, and everybody must live by those values.

FAMILY RULES

"AND THAT'S THE WAY IT IS . . . "

Society has rules. You can't drive on the left side of the road just because you want to. You can't shoot a gun off in the middle of a city block just because you feel like it. Life doesn't work that way. Neither does family life.

Drugs are against family rules. A kid can't break a rule just because he wants to or he feels like it or he thinks the rule is unfair.

Every family needs to establish a set of rules that are clear and fair and apply equitably to everyone in the family. Everybody must know up front just what the rules are. No member should ever be able to plead ignorance.

But the rules that existed for a six-year-old child will not apply when that child is eleven or fifteen—so they have to grow with the family. A six-year-old may not be allowed to cross the street by himself. An eleven-year-old may not be allowed to take his bike outside the neighborhood. A fifteen-year-old may not be allowed to attend unchaperoned parties. And so on. The rules change as the family members change and grow. But there are always rules to follow. Guidelines. Instructions, if you will. Assembling life with no set of instructions can be an awfully painful experience for an adolescent.

There are a number of standard family rules that should help you keep your children drug free. Since one of the early signs of drug-related problems is a kid's conspiracy to keep his social relationships and activities hidden from you, one of the ways to break the conspiracy is to know where your kids are and who they're with.

This does not mean you must be with your child every moment or that you must monitor every move he makes. It's simply a matter of awareness. If a child says he's going to a party, find out whose house he will be at and what time he plans to be home. By asking, you are simply showing that you care. Invite his friends over for a weekend barbecue or on a family outing. The more you get involved with his friends, the less he will be inclined to be secretive, pulling away from the family. Take time to meet the parents of his friends. If your child has nothing to hide, he will appreciate your interest. And parents who band together are the best monitoring system of all.

When a group of parents in Atlanta, Georgia, discovered that their seventh and eighth graders were experimenting with drugs—cleaning up the backyard after a thirteen-year-old girl's birthday party they found joints, pills and beer cans all over the yard—they all got together and decided to take action.

What did they do? Essentially, they shut down all communication among the kids for the rest of the summer. The kids were not allowed to see each other or talk on the phone. The KID network came to a standstill. And the PARENT network began. When the school year began, the kids were allowed to resume their regular school social life, but they were not allowed to attend any functions that did not have some of the group's parents as chaperones.

This may sound like taking extreme measures, but it worked. These were parents who took the time and energy to make sure their kids lived in a drug-free environment. They didn't pass the problem off to somebody else.

Indications are that kids are getting involved in drugs at an earlier age all the time. In 1979 we did our own study of 261 young people involved in drug treatment. At that time, only five percent said they began using drugs in the fifth and sixth grades and twenty percent said they started using in the tenth grade or later. In 1982, *only three years later,* when we repeated the survey, over twenty percent of the 350 kids questioned said they started using drugs as early as fifth or sixth grade and only two kids (not two percent, TWO KIDS!) said they started as late as the tenth grade.

Family curfews should be set for school nights and weekends, with special curfews for particular events, school proms, homecoming games, etc. Never fall victim to "everybody else's parents let them stay out 'til one A.M. Why can't I? You're so old-fashioned." That kind of guilt, applied with a shovel by a teenager, can make a parent feel like a museum piece—don't believe it for a minute. Reasonable curfews are a good family rule. Maybe some kids are allowed to stay out 'til the wee morning hours, but you probably don't want your children with them anyway. Do your own checks with other parents. Call a child's bluff when he says all the other kids do it.

The next general rule should determine what's off limits. This will probably take some research. Find out what the druggie hangouts are—usually they are video arcades, record stores, head (drug paraphernalia) shops, shopping malls, bike shops, convenience stores and certain beach, river, lake and park areas—and keep your kids away from them. Check with the local police. They will be able to give you a good idea of where druggie kids are likely to be found. There is a certain amount of drug use at all rock music concerts. And if you don't want your child tempted by drug use in a social environment, you may decide to make concerts off-limits. Of course, music is a teenager's main interest, so the best assurance you may have is to know who he is with, the kind of concert he's attending and to set a reasonable curfew.

There are enough healthy activities for children—sports, the beach, civic youth groups, church or synagogue youth groups, etc.—to make off-limits rules workable for your child. It may demand more of your time to provide transportation and supervision to these alternate places and activities, but it's worth it.

The hardest place to control a child's contact with drugs is at school. In a survey of Los Angeles Unified School District seniors, fifteen to twenty-five percent of the students said they used drugs "most of the time." Some school officials believe that figure is low. But it is consistent with figures across the rest of the nation. School officials acknowledge it. Local police departments acknowledge it. But nobody seems able to stop it.

Recently, some parents in a small town in Ohio tried. Determined to free their schools of drugs, they went to the school board and volunteered to police the school grounds, hallways and even school buses. Parents were at the school, with the students, all the time. They worked with school officials. They gave their kids a strong adult message that drugs wouldn't be tolerated in an institution for kids which adults control. It took a lot of parents a lot of time, but they did it. They were determined to provide a relatively unpressured drug-free atmosphere for their kids. And they succeeded.

If a child *does* make the decision to use drugs, he has violated a family rule, a family value, and he must understand that there are consequences for his action. He must equally understand that the reason consequences are being imposed is that he is a loved and valued member of the family.

Drugs cause turmoil in a family and the family member who brought that unrest to the family haven must face it, deal with it and accept the consequences. For teenagers, that may mean anything from no use of the car or grounding to a trip to the police station to confess. After all, drug use is not only a violation of family rules, it is also a violation of local, state and federal laws. If a trip to the police station seems necessary, a police authority should outline the law for the child and the extent of his violation. And the official should make future consequences clear. If the child should end up there again, he needs to understand the charges that he might face. It's a good idea for parents to talk to the police authority *before* taking the child in to explain the family's reasons for being there.

Consequences should be put into effect immediately. As soon as you find drugs, suspect their use, smell them, see their effects, put your punishment into action. Training a child not to use drugs is not unlike housebreaking a pet. If the newspaper across the bridge of the nose comes at the right time, the pet soon makes the association between the "fwap" on the nose and the action. Children need such rudimentary training where drugs are concerned. Think of it as the flip-side of the feel-good chemical learning sequence: the negative learning sequence says "do drugs—get punished." And again, family support is never more important than it is now. The message is, "You can do it and we are with you."

If the family drug rule is broken, you might also consider a trip to your local physician or pediatrician so that the doctor can outline for the child the effects of drugs on the body. This should be an informational experience—not a horror story. Choose a doctor who has good knowledge of drugs and strong views on adolescent drug use. It is important that the doctor knows what he is talking about, be factual and not exaggerate. Most kids will tune out any attempt at scare tactics. They have already taken drugs themselves, and they know lots of other people who do drugs regularly without leaping out of windows, committing suicide or dying with a needle in their arm. It is more important that the doctor take the time to explain the fine balance of the human body and the developmental process of adolescence and what drugs do to that balance and development. Most importantly, he should give them reliable information on the "safe drugs," alcohol, pot and coke.

After you have made the child face the consequences of his action and given him good solid information about NOT doing drugs, you need to organize the parents of your children's friends into a group effort at prevention. There's a certain amount of diplomacy needed here. Do not, repeat *do not,* call up any parent and say, "Listen, I think your little Susie may be using drugs." First of all, you're likely to get some unpleasant words and the phone slammed in your ear. But more important, you would probably shut down a chance at constructive conversation and action.

The best way to handle the situation is to call the parents of the children whom you know are your child's peers and suggest, "You know our children are growing up so fast and things have changed so much, but it's really important to me, and I know it is to you, that we keep our children safe and happy. I see some things going on around us that concern me, could we get together and talk about it?"

Get a group of parents together for coffee and dessert one evening. It's important to say what you think on *your* turf, not theirs.

It is important that both parents, not just a group of mothers, get together. When you talk to the other parents, remember what you've learned about denial and communication. Don't lecture. Don't blame. Don't say, "Your son Rick gave my daughter some marijuana." Instead, say, "I think our kids are experimenting with drugs and we need to do something about it." Shutting down the lines to other parents will not help your cause. Banding together with open eyes and ears will help everyone. Make a group plan to fight drugs.

Now, you're ready to actively involve your child in the plan to keep him straight, healthy and happy. He needs to understand why you are intervening in his drug use, and that you are willing to devote your time and attention to stopping it. He needs to know that your motivation is love and caring—not shame and embarrassment. He needs to know that you are doing it because you love him—not because it's your job or because you don't want him to have a good time or be like the rest of the kids.

Establish an activities schedule with your child. Agree to a monitoring program with him. Monitor his use of time—from household chores and homework to extracurricular and social activities. That doesn't mean that a parent has to go along on dates, but it does mean knowing that the child did in fact go to a movie and didn't just *say* he was going. It's vital that the child be actively involved in establishing this schedule. He should set his own goals and understand them. Parents and kids should go over the plan at night so that he is continually aware that there is no slack time and space. For some kids, this will mean actually laying out a schedule mapping out the day from the time he gets up until he goes to bed at night. The child who is already involved in drugs will probably require a written schedule. Other kids may be able to make better use of their time with just your encouragement and continued monitoring. What is important is that the child be involved, set his own goals and use his time constructively. Many kids who start experimenting do so because "I wonder what it's like. I don't have anything to do. I think I'll go hang out with those kids down at the beach. They always seem like they're having fun." If you have a teenager, you have undoubtedly heard him say, "I'm bored. There's nothing to do." Don't allow kids to fill the void with drugs. Fill the time void for them, help them set goals and be willing to invest the time necessary to help them attain them. "What did you do at school today, dear?" is not enough. You have to work with the child to enforce good use of time. If a child is unable to keep a schedule, to have some internal discipline, it may be a sign that drug use has already begun.

COMMUNICATION

"You must be saying something. I can see your mouth moving."

If you think you have a drug problem in your family, communication is more important than ever. A lot of parents maintain that they have open, honest communications with their kids. That they encourage them to come talk over their problems. "I tell them they can talk to me about anything." The fact is THEY don't talk to the kids about some things so the kids aren't talking to them about some things. Parents are always surprised that their children don't come talk to them about things like sex and drugs. But it shouldn't be that surprising.

A child learns open, honest communication by observation, growing up. He learns when a mother says, "Don't tell your father I let you have the car" . . . when a father says, "Answer the phone but if it's Harry, tell him I'm not home" . . . or when parents say, "Don't tell Aunt Susie what Grandma said." And the list goes on. In subtle ways, parents inadvertently teach their children more about closed, dishonest communication than they ever offset by saying, "You can talk to me about anything."

Develop a family relationship in which all family members are honest with each other. For example, instead of having your child tell someone on the telephone that you're not home, it's just as easy to say you will have to call back later. There's no reason to tell a lie. You don't have to say you're in the tub or not at home. And by being honest, you have given your child a subtle but nonetheless clear example of open, honest communications.

Similarly, family members should not keep secrets from each other. Don't tell a child that Mom has a headache and isn't coming to the family room to watch television when it's obvious that you have been arguing in the bedroom and Mom is sulking. This is not open, honest behavior and therefore, there cannot be open, honest communication. If Dad has a little too much to drink, and family members pretend it didn't happen;

or if everyone knows but no one mentions how Grandma feels about her daughter-in-law, you're setting patterns that say to a kid, there are some things this family can't talk about, and the kid in turn translates that as a reason not to talk to his family about certain aspects of his own life—particularly the controversial ones.

Learning to be honest is hard. Most people are programmed to say whatever is easiest and needs the least amount of explanation. Open communication takes more time and more thought. But if you are successful at establishing a family communication system which is truly honest, it will be a lot harder for a drug user to keep *his* secret.

Once you have learned to talk, learn HOW to talk. Communication is a skill. Funny, isn't it, how most people are careful about how they apply that skill on the job or in social situations, but they become careless at home, where it is *essential?* If you have a child involved in drugs, it may be hard for you to talk without yelling, crying, begging, accusing—but you need to learn.

All people, kids included, tend not to listen to judgmental communication. It puts the listener too much on the defensive. "Do this. Don't do that. You should do this. It's wrong to do that." As soon as communication starts, the battle lines have been drawn and everybody is set up for an argument.

Telling a child how you feel when he behaves a certain way is far more effective than yelling at him for doing it. This way, he can hear you out, and yet you have left him with the dignity to make the decision on his own to avoid making you feel that way again.

The parent who says to his child, "You never think about anybody but yourself," is lecturing. Accusing. And teenagers don't like sitting still for a sermon from the mount. The parent could just as easily have said, "I feel really angry because you're being selfish. You take care of your own needs but it ends up hurting the rest of us." By taking this kind of approach, (1) the parent has expressed how the child's actions make him feel inside, and (2) all chances for rebuttal have been closed off.

With the first example, "You never think about anybody but yourself," the child can argue that point. "I do think about you. I do care what you and Mom think." But by saying, "I feel angry because . . . ," there is no room for argument. The child cannot deny what *you* are feeling inside. He may be the expert on his behavior. But you're the expert on your feelings.

There is a simple formula for communicating feelings: "I feel _____ (use feeling word to fill in the blank) about _____ (a behavior or an event) because _____ (the reasons or explanations)." If parents learn to use this formula when they talk to their children, they are on the way to better communication.

There are many feeling words, and many varying intensities of such words. Feeling words are: angry, happy, scared, mad, sad, confused, warm, frustrated, guilty, ashamed, hurt. Consider the word "happy." A strong level of happy is elated, overjoyed or delighted. A mild level of happy is cheerful, amused or glad. And a weak form of happy is satisfied, calm or content. When you talk to your child, choose the feeling word and the intensity that best reflect what you really feel.

Conveying your inner feelings can trigger a response that a lecture, an opinion or a judgment could never evoke. Feeling messages are the basis for true interpersonal communications. Understanding each other's feelings makes people work together, live together and grow together more effectively.

But learning to talk and HOW to talk are still only part of the communications game. Now you have to learn to *listen.* Again, this is a skill that most people do better with strangers. How often does one member of your family interrupt another one? Do they finish stories for each other? Contradict one another before the first person has had a chance to complete his thought? Most people start to react verbally to another person as soon as the first three words are out of the mouth, usually because the listener has anticipated what the other person is going to say, and so plunges ahead. This interception by the listener shows a selfish need to take care of one's own interest and agenda, without regard for the other person's needs or feelings. What the listener is really reacting to is past history and past judgments, all giving him the false sense of "I know what comes next."

In families, as well as in less intimate relationships, learning to listen is a matter of listening to an entire message. You have to listen with your ears and your eyes. Watching a person's body language can sometimes tell you more about their message or their feelings than the words themselves. They illuminate the message. With teenagers, it is often easier to tell a con job by eye movement or body movement than by the convoluted story. Time, place, tone of voice, hands, facial expressions all indicate what's behind the words. The "between the lines" information—that is, what's left out—is often a clearer indication of the truth than the line itself. If you talk to your children while you're cooking dinner or washing a car, you haven't established any eye contact and are probably missing most of the message.

One of the ploys of the counseling trade is to say, "Did I hear you say . . . ?" or "Did I understand you correctly to say . . . " It's a good way of checking out communication to make sure you are truly responding to what you heard, not what you *thought* you heard.

In the parent-child relationship, there is often the "but, Mom" kind of communication. A parent will start to explain why a kid cannot go to a ball game or get a bigger allowance or go to the rock concert or smoke pot or whatever, and almost before the words are out of her mouth, the child counters, "But, Mom. . . . " The parent usually does the same kind of false communicating with solid rejoinders like "Don't 'But, Mom' me."

What is happening here is that nobody is listening to anybody. A reasonable kind of communication would have gone something like this: Daughter: "Mom, could I go to the basketball game tonight?" Mother: "No. It's a school night and you should stay home and do your homework." Daughter: "I finished my homework at school, everything but my geometry, and I can do that before time for the game."

This way each person knows where the other person stands.

Each person is responding to what the other person really is saying, not what they expected them to say. Everybody wins in this kind of communication. If the daughter is, in fact, telling the truth about the homework and not doing a con, the mother will probably decide to allow her to go to the game. There's no misunderstanding. Nobody has to slam doors or walk away feeling misunderstood.

The next step in communications is establishing closer physical contact. Somewhere along the road between childhood and adulthood, parents stop hugging their children. Fathers teach their six-year-old sons to shake hands. But six-year-old boys want to be hugged, not to shake hands. And sixteen-year-olds, just like six-year-olds and sixty-year-olds, need to be hugged, reassured, protected. Sadly, American society has come to view touching primarily as a prelude to sexual activity. Consequently, the physical manifestation of the parental nurturing role is robbed from children by the time they reach thirteen or fourteen years old. It's wrong. Hugging kids keeps love and support intact when words fail, when the interests of family members clash. It is often easier to *show* feelings than to voice them. A hug can be the warm reassurance that "you are loved" in spite of the current turbulence, and that the family is a safe, loving place to be even when you have done something wrong. In other words, hugs are as necessary for encouragement and support as they are for warmth and reward.

Once you've learned to communicate, it's time to help your child learn. Communication has to be a two-way street. Help him learn to talk, how to talk and how to listen and help him understand the value of hugging and touching. *You* need it too.

You have a far better chance of exerting a real impact on kids' lives as parents if you learn to communicate, verbally and physically . . . if you learn to talk and to listen to each other . . . if you don't hide things from your kids . . . if your behavior matches the kind of honest behavior you expect from your kids. If drugs are already in your home, you'd better catch on fast. If you have successfully avoided a drug problem so far, be thankful and take the opportunity to let family rules, understanding and communication mean drug prevention in your home.

This all may sound like a lot of work on your part. Well, it is. But it's an investment up front. Organizing a schedule, finding out where your kids are and with whom, making sure they have things to do and supervising them, *taking action* when you suspect your child has a drug problem, may seem tough, but it's a helluva lot easier than waking up one morning and finding out you've lost your child to drugs. And if you find that your own Parent Action isn't working, be willing and prepared to seek outside help immediately.

Parent Action Checklist

1. Would you recognize marijuana if you saw it? If you smelled it?
2. Are there objects in your child's room you can't identify?
3. What have you heard or seen in the news and on the street about kids and drugs in your neighborhood?
4. Is your child's peer group suddenly changing in appearance and style? Do they appear to be adopting new images, adult, sexy and sophisticated images? How do you feel about that?
5. Is your child involved in hard-rock images?
6. Is your teenager starting to test and push the limits of your family's tolerance with dress style, friends, music, activities, curfews and places to go? When he does, what happens? Does he get his way or do the family limits stand?
7. Who's in charge in your house, you or your kid? Are you afraid to lay down the law on curfew, dress or chores?
8. Does your child rush to his room when he comes home after being with friends? Does he appear nervous, sneaky or anxious to get away from you?
9. Are you afraid that the "bad kids" in the neighborhood might be influencing your kid?
10. Have your tried to have an open and calm discussion about drugs with your child? Was he evasive? Did he tell you there aren't any drugs around his school? Do you think you got anywhere? Could you sit down right now and have a frank discussion with him about drugs? Would he con you?
11. Have you been able to draw a bottom line on friends, time, music, activities or anything else, and stick with it? When your teenager starts to whine, do you give in? Does your bottom line keep changing?
12. Do you talk to your child while you're reading the newspaper, watching television or working in the garage—or do you sit down and really talk?
13. Do you think your family is in shape to spring into action

if one family member has a drug problem and needs your help?

14. *If and when your teenager gets in trouble, where would you go for help? Do you know the name of an agency or counselor who could help you decide if you have a serious problem? If it turns out to be a drug problem, what resources are available in your community for a kid in trouble with drugs or alcohol?*

7

Outside Help and Treatment
"Getting a new lease on life."

If **Parent** Action didn't work for you, there's a good chance that your child is already in Stage Two of drug use.

Stage Two will require some professional guidance, someone to help you take control of the problem as soon as possible. Don't be hard on yourself if Stage One slipped by you without your putting your foot down. Because there are no evident physical or emotional or behavioral changes in the Stage One child, it is hard for a parent to intervene.

But, as soon as you have any suspicion of a problem, don't sit around waiting for your child to admit he's using drugs. And even if he does admit to having tried drugs, remember the "ten percent rule": Whatever your child tells you is probably no more than ten percent of what he is really doing. If he admits to having tried pot once, he may be using it four or five times a week. If he admits to having smoked pot a few times he could be getting high every day. Maybe even more than once a day. It's

164

not that he's lying to you. He's denying—to you and to himself.

The sad truth is that you, the parent, may be the person least capable of determining when and if your child has a drug problem. So you will need a qualified outsider to help you make a diagnosis of your child's drug problem.

The first step in seeking outside help and treatment is the hardest—admitting that your child has a drug problem and that the problem is out of your control. It means the end of Parent Denial. It means putting an end to Kid Denial. But eventually, it may mean the end of family pain and turmoil and the beginning of a better, healthier life for the dependent child and for your family.

Don't wait until the crises build up. Don't wait to do something about it until you stand wringing your hands in a hospital emergency room. Look for the early warning signals.

And don't be afraid to admit you need help. Parents aren't qualified drug counselors. They aren't supposed to be. Don't be afraid to seek help because you're worried what the rest of your family or your neighbors will think. You're losing time. Precious time.

So get moving and do something. Stop crying yourself to sleep at night. Quit losing your temper and screaming at the kid. Quit fighting with your spouse about it. Quit pretending it will go away. Quit blaming it on the schools and the bad kids down the street. Admit you need help.

And since the situation is critical, the kind of help you find is equally critical.

HOW TO CHOOSE PROFESSIONAL HELP

"No pop psychology, please."

There is treatment available, treatment that can work. But not every person who hangs up a shingle is prepared to give you the kind of help you need. Because adolescent drug treatment is relatively new, there is a lot of trial and error going on.

Whether it is a psychologist, a social worker, a family counselor or a physician, make sure you choose a professional who believes unequivocally that drug use, all drug use, is wrong and harmful. No ifs, ands or buts.

Choose a person who believes that adults have to be responsible for children in their passage to adulthood and that children are not to be left in control of their own lives.

Never send your child to a professional without having first gone yourself. When you go, there are a couple of key questions you can ask to determine if the person is going to be helpful in your effort to save your child from drugs: (1) "Doctor, I'm confused. I've read a lot about marijuana. Some articles say it's harmful, other studies indicate it's not so harmful if it's not used in excess. I want to know what's right. Will it hurt my child or not?" (2) "Doctor, I'm really troubled. I try to be a good parent. I've read everything I can get my hands on about adolescence but it's tough. Being an adolescent isn't easy and being the parent of one is worse. I want to be fair. I want to give my child the freedom he needs to grow and experience life for himself but I don't want to give him too much freedom. He says I'm too strict on him and maybe I am. Should I respect his privacy, stay out of his room, not listen in on his phone calls? Or do I check things out for myself to make sure he's safe and telling me the truth?"

How the therapist answers these two questions will tell you whether you've got the right person. If he says, "Drug use is the symptom that something else is wrong, something else is going on with the child and needs to be examined," head for the door. DRUG USE IS A DISEASE, NOT A SYMPTOM OF A DISEASE. It is a primary disease, because it is the source of other symptoms. It is a chronic disease, because it's ongoing. It's a progressive disease because it gets worse, not better. And it's a terminal disease, because ultimately it may cause death.

If he says to you, "All kids do marijuana," get out of his office. This is a person who has accepted that marijuana use is a normal part of the adolescent experience. He has written it off as a mere social phenomenon, an evolution in adolescence like punk rock and designer jeans. You need someone who can help you see early warning signals and take corrective measures immediately.

If he laughs and says, "Hey, didn't you do any experimenting when you were growing up? All kids experiment. It's normal," hit the Yellow Pages and start looking again.

If he says, "Alcohol is not as bad as drugs. Why don't you let your kid have a drink with you once in a while . . . you know, on special occasions so he knows what it's like. Satisfy his curiosity, then you won't have so much to worry about. At least alcohol isn't dangerous," MOVE ON.

If he says things like, "You're being too tough on your kid. He's just trying out his wings . . . he can't ever learn to fly, he can't ever leave the nest, if he doesn't try some things on his own. . . . Give him the freedom to grow up. Give him the freedom to make his own decisions, right or wrong . . . he'll learn from his mistakes. Just let him take a couple of falls, he'll wise up. . . . Things aren't like they used to be. Kids are smarter. They've watched television, they've seen wars brought to them in living color at the dinner table. They've mastered computers. They've learned more in a shorter period of time than we ever did. . . . You can't protect them from the world around them. They already know about it. Trust me. You won't be disappointed," LEAVE. Don't be talked into "disco parenting" just because this guy has a degree hanging on the wall. He's living in a fantasy world. And you need reality, lots of it.

Keep looking until you find the professional who tells you that parents have to be parents and kids have to be kids. And parents have to be in charge of kids until kids become adults.

Find a person who recognizes the seriousness of drug use. A person who understands the implications of trying drugs and who is motivated to do something about it.

If in the diagnosis you determine that your child is in the early part of Stage Two, you may still be able to work with a specialist and help the child through strong Parent Action and qualified professional counseling—without putting him in a residential treatment program.

But anything past the early part of Stage Two will most likely necessitate residential treatment. If a child has started to self-medicate, it is next to impossible for you or a twice-a-week counseling session to have any impact on the chemical learning sequence.

The most important thing in achieving a drug-free child is a drug-free environment. You can't provide that and the counselor can't provide that. You can't be behind the school gym when the kids are smoking pot or in the school bathroom where the deals are being made.

One mother tried. "I didn't work so I was free to work on my child's problem when I found out he was doing drugs. And did I ever work on it. I drove him to school and picked him up. I checked every hour when he was in at home or at school and nothing worked. He kept getting worse. As a parent I really couldn't control his environment enough to keep him away from drugs once he was this far along."

You've gone this far. Don't stop now. You've already taken the two hardest steps: admitting you have a kid on drugs and admitting you need help. If your child is involved in drugs to the extent that he needs residential treatment, be prepared to seek it.

"When we left you here four days ago, it was the hardest day of my life," a Lutheran minister told his son. "I'm happy you're here and I'm happy we've made a start. I love you so much . . . son." Tears rolled down the father's face.

THE MOTHER: "I was watching you slowly kill yourself. You had become distant from us. You had become a kind of Jekyll and Hyde. I was never sure what I could say or couldn't say . . . even 'Good morning,' and know how you were going to react. You're going to make it here, I know you are, son. We want you home so badly but we want you straight and we want to be a family again."

And beware. You may run up against a specialist who tells you that your child has been using drugs for some time and that he has a serious drug problem but that he is sure he can help him with some intense sessions. He may even suggest the child come in every day after school. You're going to want to believe him. You're going to want to keep your kid home at all costs. But don't make the mistake that a father from Texas did. He spent $35,000 in counseling and hospital treatment programs (four to six weeks at a time) just so he wouldn't have to put his child in a residential drug rehabilitation program. His son is still using drugs and has now moved out of the house. The father's pride wouldn't let him admit that his child needed residential treatment. Well, he still has his pride—but he doesn't have his $35,000. Or his son.

Consider the parents who spent over $150,000 on a series of psychiatrists, psychologists, emergency rooms, medical hospitals and mental hospitals trying to find out what was wrong with their daughter—and that was after they had already wasted three years of denying that they needed help. Not one professional ever told them their daughter had a drug problem. On the contrary, one doctor asked their daughter what kind of drugs she *wanted*. One hospital gave her $950 worth of drugs in twenty-one days and another even overdosed her.

It was nine years after their battle with drugs began that this particular family finally found an adolescent drug program that helped their daughter.

Pat yourself on the back if you've come this far. If you've admitted your child is using drugs, if you've admitted you need outside help and if you admit that a residential treatment program may be the only way you're going to get your child off drugs, you're doing well. Now, you have to learn that there are all kinds of treatment programs. And you have to be as careful in choosing a program as you were in finding a specialist. What do you look for?

A Drug-Free Environment

This is not simply a place where drugs cannot get to your kid and your kid cannot get to drugs. It has to be a place where your kid can get rid of the drugs that already exist in his body.

The program should last a minimum of 90 days. Why?

Almost all kids who do drugs use marijuana, and the THC in marijuana is the hardest substance to remove from the body. You could take the worst wino off the streets and medically detox his body and have him totally free of alcohol in twenty-four hours. You could take a heroin or morphine addict and have his body entirely clear, including withdrawal effects, within four to five days. But one marijuana joint will leave THC remains in the body tissue for a minimum of fifteen days.

THC is accumulated in the body tissue because the body does not have a good method of disposing it. The result is that the body chemistry of kids who smoke four or five days a week, three to six joints a day, is never clean. The THC lodges in the fatty tissues, including the brain, and in the glandular tissues that secrete hormones, sending chemical messages to the rest of the body.

As a result, a kid on drugs may appear to be making some progress with rehabilitation and then, at the end of the 90 to 120 days it takes to clear the body of the THC, land flat on his face. The THC prevents the kid from being a thinking, feeling human being. So his mood changes may be so great that it cancels out the effects of several weeks of the therapeutic process. Only after the body is totally free of chemicals can real treatment begin. Any program shorter than ninety days is not likely to work.

A drug-free environment is the only environment in which treatment can take place. This means the removal of drugs, all drugs, all mood-altering chemicals from the child. Do *not* accept a program that wants to give your child prescription drugs to get him off illegal drugs.

Drug Use as a Disease

Find a drug program that treats drug use as a problem, *not* as a symptom of a problem. It may be true that your child's drug problems didn't start until after your divorce but this is not the time to treat the divorce. Stop the drug problem first and then help your child accept and understand the divorce.

Psychiatric units in hospitals—where many adolescent drug users end up—as well as many psychologists and psychiatrists, tend to see drug use as a symptom of something going wrong in the family or with the child himself and they end up treating the symptom while the disease runs wild. Meanwhile, druggie kids don't mind going to hospital drug units because they learn quickly how to get poorly paid orderlies to supply them with pot or alcohol.

Drug-free Lifestyle

You must find a program that helps the child develop a plan of abstinence for life. Drug use is just like alcoholism. Once an alcoholic, always an alcoholic. Once a druggie, always a druggie. Just as there is such a thing as a recovered alcoholic—a person who knows he is an alcoholic, but has decided to be alcohol free and who knows he can never again drink as long as he lives, so it is with druggies. A good treatment program doesn't sugar-coat the fact that the child who has become chemically dependent has to live with that chemical dependency for the rest of his life. That means no drugs and no alcohol. The treatment program should give the child the physical, mental and emotional help he needs to make that decision and live by it.

When kids began having problems, it caught the therapeutic community with its pants down. Nowhere was there a program qualified to help kids, little kids, break the drug habit. At first, kids with drug problems were treated in alcohol treatment units or in heroin addiction units. Both failed miserably. It was not until the mid-1970s that there were programs that specialized in treating adolescent drug use.

Chemically dependent kids cannot be treated in the same manner as adults. For the social drinker—only recently acknowledged by society as a possible alcoholic—it took ten or twelve years to develop his dependency. With a child, it takes only a matter of months, three to six, for dependency to begin.

That is why the more quickly you seek help, the better your chances of saving your child.

Family Treatment

A good program requires involvement by and treatment for all family members. Remember, drug use is a family systems disease. Without treatment, siblings of a drug user become high risks for drug involvement themselves. The family of the user has become used to enabling and, without treatment themselves, they will continue to enable the user. Treatment for family members is the way to stop them from being part of the problem . . . and make them part of the solution. To help the drug-dependent child get better, and make intervention and treatment work: (1) The parent has to come to terms with his own feelings about chemical dependency, the use of alcohol and drugs. (2) A parent has to become knowledgeable about drugs, what they do to the body, what they look like and how they are used. (3) A parent has to separate his own feelings of self-worth from his kid's. The parent who says to himself, "I screwed up as a parent or my kid wouldn't be on drugs. I want to hide this. I hope nobody finds out," is not going to be honest and open in the rehabilitation process. (4) There can be no family conspiracies. Mom cannot conspire with a sibling to hide something from Dad just to keep him from getting mad and running up his blood pressure. Kids cannot conspire against parents. And parents cannot conspire against kids. The whole family must care enough to protect each other, through honesty and working together.

Peer Counseling

As Alcoholics Anonymous and other rehabilitation programs have found, "those who have the problem" can best be helped by "others who have the problem and are recovering." The same is true of adolescent drug treatment. Given the peer pressure involved in getting a kid to use drugs, a good treatment program turns peer pressure to its advantage. Peers are particularly good in working with the adolescent age group because they are much less easily conned than adults. Kids who have been there themselves can separate the truth from the fiction and help break the denial process. It's the "you-can't-con-a-con" approach.

Treatment Tools

Many programs utilize some version of the Alcoholics Anonymous Tools of Change as a basis for adolescent treatment. AA Tools which are effective for adolescent use include: (1) *Admit I am powerless over drugs and come to believe that a power greater than myself can restore me to sanity.* This simply means that a child has to accept that he is not in control of the drugs but that drugs have taken control of him and that he needs help in order to change. (2) *Make a decision to turn my will and my life over to the care of God as I understand him.* Now that the child has admitted having a problem, he must decide to do something about it. He may try to regain control of his life by believing and putting his faith in God or the universe, a strong value system, his family, or another human being—whatever works for him. (3) *Make a searching and fearless inventory of myself daily.* Each day a child will take a serious look at his problem and then set goals to help solve the problem. The expression that grew out of AA, "one day at a time," also applies here. This is designed to help give an improved sense of self-control and help rebuild self-esteem. Kids first learn to set small goals, goals that they can handle, daily goals, and then they can move on. (4) *Admit to God, myself and another human being the exact nature of my wrongs, immediately.* Simply put, this is the hallmark of the end of denial, a crucial step in the therapeutic process. The druggie kid who starts admitting to himself and to others what drugs have done to his life is on the way to a new beginning. (5) *Make direct amends to such people where possible except when to do so would injure them, myself or others.* Learning to say "I'm sorry" for the pain that his drug use may have caused is part of the reconstruction of values that a recovering druggie must go through and learning to repair the damage that his drug use has caused is necessary to regain his self-respect. (6) *Having received the gift of awareness, I will practice these principles in all my daily affairs and carry the message to all that I can help.* This means living one's life in such a way that a strong sense of values and quality is passed on to others.

An Intensive Therapy Process

The best programs are ones that offer strong, structured therapy. What may appear on the surface to be militaristic or authoritarian is the best way to bring reason and order back into the chaotic druggie lifestyle. You can't treat cancer with aspirin, right? And you can't treat drug use with simple rap sessions. Some programs feature a group meeting a day, a little individual counseling, and lots of free time for TV, ping-pong and hanging around. The effective programs keep kids busy at therapeutic tasks from dawn until bedtime. The combination of structure and filled time helps young people fight back the compulsion to get high. The good programs have regular mealtimes, and the balance of the day is filled with scheduled activities, including group therapy, individual therapy, AA meetings, planned recreational activities and educational groups concerning alcohol, drugs and chemical dependency. Druggie kids need a structured environment in which to reorient themselves. They have lost all goals, all structure, all focus, all basis of reality in their lives, so the more quickly some sort of order is introduced, the sooner they will get their footing. Don't be one of those parents who rushes in and says, "You're being too hard on my child." That's enabling. Your little darling is going to suffer less in the hands of a qualified drug counselor than he will on the streets doing drugs with his friends. Parents often take their children out of treatment programs because they can't stand seeing their children put through the regimen that most drug programs demand. That's the worst thing a parent could do. It automatically says to the child that the parent is going to protect him from all the big, bad consequences of drug use. The therapy program has to be intensive and structured to work. Be prepared not only to expect it but find a program that offers it.

Social Reintegration

Good programs help adolescents progressively reconstruct all areas of their lives including family, school, friendships, leisure time and dating. But successfully returning to those areas of the adolescent lifestyle requires strong and continuous monitoring from the treatment system itself. Kids cannot be expected to survive if they are returning to their old, uncontrolled environment without support. A good program limits the areas in which a child tests his new tools of handling events and feelings. The first arena is usually the family. The child leaves the residential phase of treatment and returns to living at home, where he has to cope with the stresses of family life and face the family issues that may have resulted from his drug use. When he is successful in that arena, he moves on to the next, in which he must learn to operate is his peer group, and that usually means returning to school. This point of his social reintegration may be the hardest and most tempting. Therefore, it requires strenuous monitoring on the part of the treatment program. And so it goes. One by one, the child faces each phase of his life. There may be additional snags when he has to make his own decisions about what to do with his leisure time—the space people usually fill with things that make them feel good and therefore a potentially tempting opportunity for a druggie kid to call up that old learning sequence with, "Screw it, I can fill this time by getting high." It is for those times that treatment workers have to be standing by, ready to yank on the leash, pick kids up by the nape of the neck, dust them off and start them over in the recovery process. Opening the doors of a treatment center and sending a kid out on the street like Edward G. Robinson leaving the prison is not realistic. Children have to be given responsibility a little at a time.

It's essential to remember that drugs have interrupted the maturation process. The adolescent passage from childhood to adulthood has been stopped in midstream, by drug use. That is why it is not unusual to find a 17-year-old drug user who has the maturity of a thirteen-year-old. The treatment process should help get the druggie kid back on his developmental journey by helping him identify questions and find answers. "Who am I? How do I see myself? How do I want other people to see me?" The question of sexual identity also needs to be addressed and the treatment process can help the child answer such sexual identity questions as "How do I see myself as a male or female? How do I see myself in relationship to members of the same sex? How do I see myself in relationship to members of the opposite sex?"

The treatment process should help the child develop coping mechanisms—the internal tools that help the child deal with the ups and downs of life once it is no longer appropriate for parents to do the coping for him. Internal tools help a person cope with change without losing his basic stability. To function as a healthy person, adults have to develop the internal emotional equipment to soar from life's peaks to its valleys without losing their emotional balance. Teenagers, prone to radical mood swings, also need to learn how to handle emotional swings without coming unglued at the seams. But the adolescent on drugs quickly learns that when he hits a valley, drugs will take him to the next peak. What treatment has to offer is the wherewithal to face emotional change without drugs—and with internal emotional strengths.

The drug user has to admit that drugs are controlling him and they are ruining his life before he can start a substantive reconstruction of his life.

The beginning of treatment is like an excavation project, helping kids dig up all their old behavior, the trouble the behavior got them in and the resulting bad feelings that have been suppressed. In treatment, kids need to dig up those buried feelings. They need to talk about their past, about their behavior, about the pain, the shame, the guilt that went along with their drug use. They need to talk to other kids who've been there about what drugs made them do; they need to reveal their feelings to kids who will force them to deal honestly and openly with the hurt that they have buried deep inside. When kids start to talk about the painful, difficult things in their past, the feelings that they have repressed, that's when the real recovery process begins.

At some point, a kid will begin to see the connection between drugs and pain. "I did all those things. I overdosed. I behaved terribly. I got in trouble. I embarrassed people who care about me and whom I care about. And I felt bad about it. Hey, I see my problem. The drugs really were ruining my life." This discovery by the adolescent drug user is best done in an environment with peers who are also recovering and understand, and who can help in that journey from deception and denial to openness and honesty.

Once all those bad feelings have been dug out, the child then faces the problem of dealing with his guilt. The treatment process cannot open a wound and leave the victim bleeding. A good program must also help the child face the guilt associated with doing drugs and the guilt of the immoral behavior that resulted from his drug use. The best way to do that is to have kids who have already started to deal with the same kinds of guilt, kids who are further along in the recovery process, help the child understand that *drugs* caused the problem, not a flaw in his personality. And kids need to help each other learn that *because* drugs caused the behavior and *because* they are not going to go back to drugs, they are not going to go back to that unacceptable behavior. So, they can forgive themselves. To get on with life, it is necessary to forgive oneself, to absolve the guilt and move forward. The treatment process should make the child understand that he is not made of indecent fiber and that he can start a life that is drug free, ethical and moral whenever he decides to move forward. And moving forward includes doing what he can to make up for all the pain and hurt that he has put other people through.

Why is it so crucial that the guilt be erased? Because guilt is the foundation for shame, and shame is bad feelings about one's self. Kids who have been on drugs will often have amassed so many bad feelings that they feel "like a piece of crap. Why try to change—I'm no good anyway." Changing, getting rid of that shame, means developing a sense of hope and gives the kid a chance to start again and to regain control of his life, one day at a time. He sets goals, small goals, day by day, and works to attain them. The exercise is designed to help kids learn to make changes, to give kids a sense of regaining control, thereby rebuilding their self-worth and self-esteem. Once the past is faced and accepted, the child will be able to learn the skills necessary to remain drug free and to control his thoughts, feelings and behavior.

TREATMENT SUMMARY

Let's reexamine the points of intervention and the type of treatment that is likely to be needed at each stage of drug use.

As you have already learned, the best time to catch drug use is in Stage One, when the child is using only on weekends, under peer pressure and when someone else is providing the substance. At most the child will have tried alcohol, pot and inhalants. There has been no detectable change in his behavior.

Parents who intervene at this point have a good chance of doing something about the problems themselves. Certainly this is true if they get a good diagnosis from a qualified professional and guidance on how to deal with the situation. But unless you get lucky, happen upon it and catch the kid in the act, you're never going to know it.

So your next best move is to intervene when the child is in early Stage Two of drug use. That's when parents start to feel uneasy about their child without quite knowing why. Curfews get ignored. There are mild changes in appearance. The teenager is bubbling with enthusiasm one minute and slamming doors and screaming the next. The parent feels irritated and threatened but at a loss as to what's going on. The instinct is to write it off to squirting hormones, but the truth is you're experiencing the first mood swings of drug use.

The child has learned to feel good from drugs and has started to seek out drugs to get high. But the discomfort of coming down is now occurring for the first time.

The parent who intervenes at this point will need more outside help than the parent who moved in on Stage One. But early in Stage Two, parents have a decent chance of helping the child while he still lives at home and continues going to school. The early Stage Two druggie still has it within his ability to make the decision to change. The early Stage Two parent, however, must have good professional guidance. This parent must make the time for strong adult supervision in every phase of the child's life. The family must work on good communication, a strong set of family rules, values and bottom lines, and must implement strong consequences when family rules are broken, values violated and bottom lines crossed. Helping the Stage Two child will be a full-time job. If the child has already moved into later Stage Two, if the child has learned to self-medicate, to make bad feelings go away with drugs, only a residential program is likely to help.

Most parents will resist residential treatment but the late Stage Two kid is heading for Stage Three at breakneck speed and it's unlikely that doctors, counselors and parents can work fast enough to win the race against drug deterioration. Of course, the need for treatment varies with every child and every parent. And every parent wants to think his is the family that can do it on their own. What parents lose sight of is the influence of the environment outside the home and the fact that the child they know, the one they think has the discipline, the values and the self-worth to stop this whirling cesspool, is not in control. The drugs are in control. The best and surest help for the late Stage Two child is a residential program.

The parent who fails to stop the Stage Two child is going to face disaster. The Stage Three drug user gets in trouble at school repeatedly, runs away from home, attempts suicide.

This child has moved from stealing the five-dollar bill out of Mom's purse to shoplifting, breaking and entering and perhaps even auto theft. He admits to trying drugs and expounds a philosophy that "marijuana is no worse for you than tobacco or alcohol."

By the time a druggie kid reaches Stage Four of drug use (and remember this whole four-stage process can take place in a matter of weeks, or months, not years), he is probably not living at home. He is living on the street and taking drugs every day. He is no longer taking drugs to feel good. He now has to have drugs all the time just to feel normal, just to get out of bed, just to move aimlessly through a day. The only time a parent is likely to hear from a Stage Four druggie is when he breaks into the house to get clothes or take food or steal something he can sell to get money to buy more drugs or when the police call and tell the parents to come get their kid out of jail again or when the hospital calls to find out who's going to be responsible for paying the bills when the kid overdoses one more time. By now, parents think of their child as a living corpse. They have given up on him. It's the only way parents of the Stage Four druggie have of going on with their lives. It's not that they wish the child were dead (although some parents admit there are times when they think their child would be better off dead), it's more a matter of living with the pain.

The message for Stage Four parents from people who work in drug rehabilitation is, "Hey folks, don't give up. Your child can recover. It's going to be a long, slow painful process. But it's worth it." And parents are the only people who care enough to take that long painful trip with their child. Druggie friends don't care. Cops and anybody else who might cross the child's path think he's a lost cause. But it's worth it to take that chance —the only chance, the last chance—to save the kid.

Again, the point of intervention and the accuracy of the diagnosis are the keys to finding the right treatment. And the right treatment is successful treatment, treatment that not only produces a drug-free child but treatment that gives him the ability to remain drug free.

To summarize: a treatment program should offer (1) a totally drug-free environment in which your child can recover, (2) peers who can identify with the pain and hurt of drug use, both in the rehabilitation process and as counselors, (3) an emphasis on facing the past, acknowledging what drugs have done to the child's life, and dealing with it, (4) ways of rebuilding a child's self-worth, (5) counseling for other family members and (6) the coping mechanisms to face tomorrow drug free.

What that should achieve, if successful, is a child who is drug free, a child who is dealing with his past, a child who has a sense of self-esteem and a child strong enough to operate in all areas of the normal adolescent passage.

But no drug program in this country is 100 percent successful. Drug programs lose kids every day. They run away. They go back to druggie friends. They go back to getting high. They overdose. They attempt suicide. And sometimes they die. The treatment process is not one that comes with a lot of gold stars to mark successes. There are victories, many of them, and they come in all different sizes and shapes . . . the tall, tan, dark-haired boy who is heading off to college, who feels good about himself and talks about future goals . . . the shy little girl with freckles who's gone back to being a little girl. It's the parent who beams with pride, so glad to have his child back, so glad to have a second chance. It's the brother who says, "Ted, I'm really proud of you. I know maybe I never told you. But I love you, Ted, I really do."

The average drug rehabilitation program for adolescents has a success rate of less than twenty percent. Some have been able to make great strides in helping kids and helping families. Even in one of the most successful rehabilitation programs in the country, the percentage of kids who remain drug free for at least a year after treatment is only about sixty percent. Walking out the door drug free is not enough. Success means *staying* drug free.

Getting treatment does not mean getting a guarantee. There's no warranty card. What treatment does offer is hope. Hope for the child. Hope for the family. And hope for the future.

Outside Help and Treatment Checklist

1. Have you tried Parent Action and it failed?
2. Is your child changing in negative ways at school and home, in terms of his peer group, his appearance and his physical health?
3. Has your child admitted trying marijuana?
4. Are you experiencing feelings from anxiety to pain because your child and family life seem to be getting out of control?
5. Do you feel like you need help?
6. Are you constantly arguing with your kid about limits—curfews, clothes, etc.?
7. Are you and your spouse regularly at odds over control and discipline of the child?
8. Is your child starting to question by word and behavior the family's values?
9. Do you have an uneasy sense that things are getting worse?
10. Are you starting to look for reasons why it isn't drugs?
11. Are school officials, neighborhood friends or church workers suddenly showing discomfort and/or concern about your child?
12. Is your child starting to withdraw from and avoid the family?
13. Has your child started to skip school, steal, defy you, stay out at night, and have your efforts at management totally failed?
14. Has the home situation become so painful that you have to do something?
15. Have you tried parent control and it failed?
16. Have you tried psychologists and psychiatrists and they failed?
17. Have you tried outpatient drug treatment and it failed?
18. Are you afraid nothing will work?

19. *Do you live with constant anxiety waiting for the next disastrous crisis from your child?*
20. *Have you given up on your child?*
21. *Do you sometimes wish your child were dead?*

8

Prevention

"No warranty. No refunds. No money-back guarantees."

If you're like most parents, you'd give anything to hear that the scientific community had come up with a cure for kids on drugs. Wouldn't it be great if you could turn on your television and see Dan Rather say, "Good evening. Tonight's top news story . . . the drug epidemic has ended. Government sources today announced a shutdown of all illegal drug trafficking in this country."

Well, sorry, but this isn't likely to happen. There are no magic elixirs out there. The government hasn't been able to stop illegal drug trafficking. And drugs are no more likely to disappear from a teenager's environment than Big Macs, french fries and pizza.

It would be nice if this book could provide you with some assurances. "If your child is _____ or _____, you don't have a thing to worry about." The sad truth is: THERE ARE NO GUARANTEES. There are no vitamins that, if taken daily, are going to prevent the disease. And there's nothing about your child that makes him invincible in the face of drugs.

So the best you can hope for is your own not-so-magic elixir, a family potion, a kind of prevention that, while it still will give you no guarantees or immunities, will give you fighting strength. It's being prepared to wage a war you hope you never have to fight. It's called Prevention.

Prevention is a safety measure. It's like keeping matches away from small children, locking up poisonous substances and putting nonskid mats under rugs. It's something you do to provide your family with the happiest and safest environment possible. But prevention against drug use is not easy—especially when psychological and sociological experts are talking about the failure of the family in our precarious times. It's hard for the family to stand as a bulwark against the ever increasing influence of school, peers and the media.

You've learned that families are the basic unit of loving and caring, of strength and stability. That, while families may bounce aimlessly around when family members have problems, they can also be resilient, like super rubber balls, if other family members understand and reach out to stabilize the disturbance, rather than grabbing balance by finding new family roles. You've learned that family members working together can rebound. And you've learned that healthy families are the best prevention.

PARENTAL PATTERNS
"LIKE FATHER, LIKE SON."

Prevention starts with you, the parent. Parents teach the infant his first learned reactions—smiling, laughing, and cooing. It is parents who set the learning pattern, and that pattern continues into adulthood.

But we don't mean to imply that parents and family systems cause kids to become involved with drugs. As we've said repeatedly, *kids* make the decision to try drugs the first time and to use drugs with their friends again and again before they finally lose control and become dependent. What *is* true is that certain issues can cause communication problems within a family, thereby lessening the influence of parents at the times when kids are most susceptible to the lure of drugs. Kids also learn patterns of coping with life from parents that either help them resist peer pressure or make them more vulnerable to it. But, again, there's no magic formula: Many kids who've been protected from peer pressure by their parents still become involved with drugs, and many unsupervised kids somehow manage to say no to drugs. But let's look closely at what parents can do anyway.

Kids' "beauty marks" as well as their "warts" come from the parents. Parents like to claim the strengths and pass on the weaknesses. A mother will say her son gets his bad temper from his father. Or a father will say his daughter gets her stubborn streak from her mother. If it's a pleasant personality or musical talent, suddenly everybody is willing to lay claim to it. The fact is, parents are role models for both the strengths *and* the weaknesses in their children. Consciously and unconsciously, parents pass on family values and behavior.

Parents knowingly hand down their values—family traditions, strong feelings about how children should act, what schools they should go to, what professions are admirable ones, what their life values should be, what spiritual beliefs they may have and so forth. Moms and dads live, speak and act out their conviction in these values every day. A child may willingly accept some of them, and may see others as enormous pressures. Dad may really want his son to follow in his footsteps and go to Yale. The child may end up spending most of his school years just wondering if he can measure up and be accepted at his old man's alma mater. But the parents don't want the child to be pressured. They simply want him to have strong religious beliefs. They want him to go to college. They want him to carry on family traditions. Their intentions are usually the best. But unknowingly, they pass along just as many negative traits from the growing-up war chest as positive ones. They may unknowingly pass along an unspoken fear of touching or hugging. Or the inability to say, "I love you." Parents are pattern-makers. Don't forget it.

CARRY-OVER ISSUES

"Excess baggage."

Every person carries into a new relationship his own personal family "heirlooms." Within the family, a parent comes into the new parent-child relationship with his own set of baggage, a series of issues packed away in his mind and actions, and as soon as any new relationship—whether it's a child, lover, friend or spouse—becomes familiar, it's time to unpack the bags and slip on the old, tired, comfortable attitudes. These attitudes may appear tattered and unacceptable to others, but they belong to you and you hang onto them for dear life. No matter how unattractive they may be, you wear them around the house for everyone to see.

Let's consider some examples. If a parent remembers his childhood as a concentration camp because his own parents may have been extremely strict or stern or even physically abusive, a parent is likely to respond in one of two ways. He might (1) choose to run his own home like a concentration camp out of reverence to his own parents or simply because it's what he knows. Even if the memories are bitter, he may rationalize, "I turned out all right. I thought it was tough at the time but it was really good for me. And if it was okay for me, it's okay for my kids." Or he may be so bitter about the experiences that he may (2) react by going as far in the other direction as possible: "It was hell for me and I never want my kid to go through anything like it. I want my kid to have a better time of it than I did." This parent overcompensates for everything, giving the child everything—except firm guidance and control and bottom lines.

Both reactions are extreme. Neither is an example of good parenting. Neither will produce a teenager with healthy feelings of self-worth.

The dissatisfied parent is not the only example. A parent may have looked up to his own parents or liked the way he was treated as a child so much that he does everything he can to replicate that relationship with his own child. He does this out of a sense of well-being and because he wants to get back in touch with the affection, warmth and security *he* felt as a child. This behavior grows out of good memories. Regardless of your motivation, you, as a parent, cannot base the way you deal with your children on whatever unresolved issues you have with your own parents. Your child is a real live human being —not a little carbon copy of you. He's part of you and part of another person and parts of a lot of generations before. He is a self-conscious "I" with feelings and needs that don't have one thing to do with what went on between you and your parents. You can never impose the past over the present—especially your past over someone else's present. You are not your parents. Your child is not you as a child. The world is different. The setting is different. You can't go back. If you try, your child will balk. He won't understand how the same rules apply. Whatever growing up was like to you—whether you had to walk to school, or hold down a job to help the family get by—it means nothing to your child except another boring story he can't relate to. He can't feel your bad experiences. The best you can hope for from your memories is to pass along the results of your growing up, as measured by what you are today.

So remember: (1) Your child cannot be placed in the position of having to fulfill your unfulfilled ambitions. If you were a second-string guard, don't expect your child to become a star quarterback. If you couldn't win the dance recital competition, don't expect your child to earn a place in the Joffrey Ballet. You can't relive your past by vicariously living your child's present. (2) You cannot obsessively protect your child from mistakes you made yourself. A mother cannot be compulsive about a daughter's dating because she got pregnant and had to get married. A father cannot force a son into an education because he feels that his own lack of education trapped him in an unfulfilling job. (3) It is tempting to envision your child following in your footsteps and doing the same things that were your own best successes . . . going to the same school, joining the same fraternity, playing the same musical instrument, excelling in the same sport, winning the same school office, entering the same profession, taking over the family business. Parents like to have their children repeat their own triumphs—out of feelings of selfishness and safety. It's selfish because it's merely a way of extending the limits of your own life. And it feels safe because the events of your own life are a beaten and familiar path.

It's all right to have learned from your successes and failures. It's not all right to apply your wants and needs, your fears and triumphs, to your unsuspecting and vulnerable child.

Use your history as experience, make it relevant in forming judgments, establishing rules and relating to your own child and other children; but don't expect your childhood to be any more than a reference guide for you. Combine it with all the other experiences, past and present, to make your relationship with your child strong and relative. Don't get caught up in trying to deal with your child's problems in ways that have to do with either happy memories or unresolved angers of your own. It's not fair—to you or your child.

Take an inventory. In dealing with your child, how many times do you, either out loud or in your head, refer to your own parents or your childhood as "the good old days"? Make a list of the issues that trigger "the way we were" responses in you and then set out to resolve those issues. Figure out what it is from your past that makes you upset, angry, depressed or afraid and then give those things a decent burial. Sometimes resolving old issues may require a visit to a qualified therapist, but it is worth it to set yourself, your child and your family free of the weight of excess baggage.

CHEMICAL DEPENDENCY

"IT'S BAD BUT PASS IT ON ANYWAY."

Did your mother or your father have a problem with alcohol or prescribed drugs? What about a grandparent? Do you remember your parents talking about a certain member of the family who liked his liquor and had to have "a little nip" from time to time, or how someone behaved when he was drinking?

If so, it's very possible that you may have a chemically dependent child, and chemical dependency is a family disease. It can be passed on. Alcoholism has been considered a family disease for some years, and there is evidence that a small number of alcoholics have a genetic tendency toward alcoholism—the first drink triggering compulsive and out-of-control drinking patterns.

The majority of alcoholics and drug users, however, are not genetically predisposed to dependency. In their cases, the family disease is emotional, psychological, and is carried from generation to generation through the family system. Most studies in this area deal with alcoholics and not drug users, but they do indicate that members of chemically dependent families have a higher incidence of alcoholism and stress-related physical and mental illnesses than other families.

The dependency seems to be focused in the areas of compulsive behavior, feelings and self-worth. Drug use in a family causes each individual to become radically self-centered in an effort to survive under the high stress and pain of the family, and subsequently to become engaged in compulsive behavior in defense against that pain. Gradually, the compulsive behavior builds a wall around the person's identity and causes feelings to be held in, suppressed or frozen. The effect of all of this is to create fragile or declining feelings of self-worth. One of the ways to cope with the stress, the turmoil, one's own compulsive behavior, the lack of self-worth is to turn to alcohol or drugs.

Drugs are shaking new family trees. The advent of adolescent drug use has created a number of new carriers of the chemical dependency disease. For many families, a child using drugs is the first carrier of the disease in that family's history. When you consider the increase in the number of families carrying this disease, willing it down from generation to generation (unless they are treated), this is indeed an ominous sign.

If you've had drug dependency or alcoholism in your family, even though you may not be addicted, you are a "carrier." You are the contagion in your family and you can produce it again in your kids. Remember, genetics is not the only way of passing on family traits. If you take a survey of your family tree and find chemical dependency, then you should go to a place like Al-Anon or a local alcoholism treatment agency to learn more about chemical dependency. You may find that you need treatment yourself to stop being a carrier of the disease.

Chemical dependency in your family history may have had an effect on you. It may have programmed you to act or react to various family and social situations. And, overtly or covertly, you may be doing something to activate your own child's use. If you had an alcoholic parent or a drug-dependent parent, your memories of it may be so painful that you are unable to talk rationally about alcohol and drug use; maybe you even become irrational any time the subject comes up. Your overreaction to old fears and hurts may be your way of reaching out to protect your children from the problems you saw and felt. But if your child does not understand your motivations, he may react to your overreacting by self-medicating himself. "What's all the fuss about? I think I'll try and find out." What you perceive as caring, your child may perceive as scaring, if you don't take time to understand—and help your child understand your own motivations.

COMMUNICATING BAD FEELINGS

"IT'S TIME FOR AN 'I' EXAMINATION."

Communicating bad feelings within the family sets a kid up to do drugs. Remember the mobile illustration. Just like the druggie kid who shakes the family mobile to search for a new balance, parents can also shake the family mobile. If the parents are unhealthy individuals, the tendency is for the family mobile to be always off balance. The rules are bad. The roles people play are bad. And the feelings are bad. The result is that a kid who is part of the family mobile that cannot find a proper balance feels bad. It doesn't feel warm and good and healing and growing to be part of this family, and kids who feel bad try drugs to feel good and get hooked on drugs pretty quickly once they are exposed. Take a look at your family mobile. Does it seem out of balance more often than not? Is there something you or your spouse or another member of the family is doing to bring bad feelings into the family? Are there unresolved issues that throw off the family balance? If so, you probably need to do a little pruning, trimming and fertilizing to make your family tree a healthy one.

You can start by taking a look at yourself. How balanced is your life as an individual? Do you feel generally satisfied or dissatisfied with your life? Do you feel like a success or a failure? That doesn't mean that you have to feel satisfied and successful all the time. Everybody has periods of feeling frustrated and dissatisfied with their lives. That's where the energy to grow, improve and move ahead comes from. But, as a whole, do you have good feelings about your life? If you don't, you probably communicate those bad feelings to your child every day. And the child who watches a parent feel bad about life may feel bad about life himself. And the child or parent who feels bad about his own life is more likely to self-medicate to feel good. Bad feelings are communicated. And bad feelings are a direct, if not scenic, route to drug use.

Human beings function in a number of areas that contribute to their own feelings of self-worth. The first is one's inner feelings, how we feel about who we are, internal peace with one's self and one's values. The second has to do with how one person sees himself in relationship to the rest of the family. Does he contribute to the total self-worth of the family? Does he perform his role in balance with the rest of the roles in the family? Are other family members happy to have him as part of the family? The next area of self-worth has to do with external goals: achievement, education, job, appearance and public service. The person who sets his own educational and job goals and achieves them is likely to feel better about himself than the person who has let himself down in terms of failing at educational and career goals. The person who never sets or attains goals is likely to carry some frustration that will translate into a negative sense of self-worth. A person's feelings about himself are also based on his ability to deal with other people, not only family and friends but business and community relationships as well. This, of course, is tied to the other levels of self-worth. Because, as you might imagine, the person who feels good about himself, his family relationships, and is satisfied with his external goals will have the confidence and the strength to relate to others.

Your appearance is a vital aspect and manifestation of your sense of self-worth. It shows the care you have for yourself to family members and to strangers. Just as the druggie kid begins to neglect his own hygiene when drugs destroy his self-worth, a parent indicates to others his lack of self-respect if his appearance is neglected or treated as unimportant. This is not to say that a person has to be beautiful to have strong feelings of self-worth, but a person needs to be concerned with his outer appearance, because it is a direct message to others about inner feelings.

The final area of self-worth is responsibility to society, how a person sees himself in relation to the world around him. Does he contribute to the world he lives in and does he do anything about making it a better place to live in for himself and for everybody else? This can include anything—from not littering the landscape to being concerned about nuclear war. It means caring for the whole of society—not just your little corner of it.

What all that means to you as a parent is that in order for you to bring your own balance into the family mobile, you have to first examine you. Are you happy with your inner feelings, your family relationships, your external goals, your social relationships and your societal responsibility? If you answer yes in all of these areas of self-worth, you are doing something right and are bringing a good strong role model to your family and a good steady balance to the family mobile. You are way ahead in the prevention game if you can provide this kind of stability to yourself, your child and your family. If you answered no in any area of self-worth, try to figure out why. Your negative feelings are no doubt being passed on to your family. And again, communicating bad feelings can set your child up to do drugs.

Once you've examined your sense of self-worth, you need to take a look at the dimensions of what it takes to make up a total human being. There are three facets to every person: the body, the mind and the spirit. Your physical side carries around the other two. It's the bag of skin and superstructure of bones that allows the other two to exist. You're used to hearing a lot about keeping in shape—jogging, dieting, stopping smoking and so forth, all ways for you to take care of your physical self. The second you is your mental side—it decides who you are, what you know and how you use it to reach to the outside world. It includes growing, learning, planning, fantasizing, dreaming and feeling. In recent years, people have become more involved in their mental health, their happiness, and how it relates to their total being. It also includes willpower, the force of personality to make decisions about one's best interest and the ability to carry through those decisions. Healthy willpower is often called assertiveness. Assertiveness is not negative. Aggression is negative. Assertiveness is taking care of yourself in positive ways without hurting others in the process. There are two forms of willpower: (1) the ability to say yes to things you want and need and (2) the ability to say no to other things and other people who violate your needs. The third facet to the total human being is the spiritual side—the least understood and often the most neglected part of a person's well-being. One's spiritual dimension is that which is outside of and higher than "self." Depending upon one's background and upbringing, a person may have strong religious ties or none. He may be so devout as to spend his life in God's service or he may be an atheist. Chances are your spiritual self probably falls somewhere in between—and you probably devote far more time and energy to your physical and mental health than to your spiritual health. Once you decide how you feel about this area of your life, think about whether you actually put that belief into practice.

So the beginning of prevention for your child is to check out you. Then the next thing is to check out other family members. How does each family member see his inner feelings, his family relationships, his external goals, his social relationships and his societal responsibility? Do each of you give adequate attention to your own physical, mental and spiritual well-being? Assess each one. Good prevention demands that you examine all areas of each family member's life. You might be surprised to discover, for example, that your daughter is having a hard time with social relationships. This could be a cue to you that she is having problems with her own self-worth and is looking for acceptance by her peers. As you learned in the chapter on Kid Denial, peer pressure is the single biggest reason for a child experimenting with drugs. So you, the parent, should be concerned when you discover a child unhappy in her other social relationships. Chances are the child is either already trying or is at least considering trying drugs in order to gain peer acceptance. The child who feels like a failure because he is not reaching his external goals may need some extra time and attention from you to get his self-worth back in shape. Remember, the child who feels bad about any one of the given levels of self-worth, or about any one of the three facets of his well-being, is likely to be in search of something to make those bad feelings turn into good feelings. And that something could well be drugs or alcohol.

The three facets of human beings—the physical, the mental and the spiritual—come in kid sizes too, and children need to develop a balanced trinity in their own lives, based on examples set by the parents. Be involved with your children in their physical conditioning. Encourage it. Don't be put out because of the time you have to devote to track or swimming meets. The discipline required for body development is worth encouraging in your child. Take an interest in his intellectual growth—not just in terms of his classroom education but the education he gets at home and in the community. Most kids are naturally curious. Encourage your child to develop his inquiring mind. Encourage him to develop interests on several levels. The child who is only interested in math or science is less likely to have as strong a sense of self-worth as the child who is interested in math, music, science *and* model airplanes. Give him as much exposure to various learning opportunities as you can afford and as your community provides. If you check with local libraries, college extension programs and art schools, many offer workshops for young children. Talk about your faith with your children, how it developed and where you think it will take you. Encourage their questions and try to expose them to other viewpoints within your faith. The stronger a child's sense of self-worth, the stronger he is physically, mentally and spiritually, the more equipped he is to face down the temptation of experimenting with drugs to feel good. Because he may already feel good.

Each family member should know that you are assessing his or her life with this three-by-five standard (three facets of well-being, five levels of self-worth). Explain it to them one night at dinner or around the family room. If family members know you are making an attempt to understand them—their strengths *and* their weaknesses—they will know that you love and care about them. If any family member is reluctant to reach out halfway in this attempt at family understanding and balance, you have probably touched upon a sensitive area that you will need to focus on. Make it clear to everyone that you are applying this same three-by-five standard to yourself—even more stringently than to anyone else—and that you need their help, support and observations. Once under way, this program can become a subject of ongoing family conversation and participation. It can even be fun!

With this kind of active family prevention program, you encourage family health—and discourage family disease.

THE COUPLE RELATIONSHIP

"UNITED WE STAND, DIVIDED WE FALL."

Having dealt with you the individual and with family members, it is time to examine the "we"—the couple relationship, which You, as parents, as a couple, are the next layer in the family superstructure. The health of your family has to do with your commitment to each other. It has to do with shared values and goals. With providing a "we, the couple" leadership for the family rather than a rooming-house atmosphere, where lives intermingle without an anchor or central focus. A strong couple relationship is a sound, secure foundation for children. Knowing their parents care about and support each other and can deal with disagreements is the best security for kids learning how to relate to parents and to each other. Check out your couple relationship. Do you really know each other? Are you competitive? Do you support each other as individuals and in the parent relationship? Can your kids feel secure in your commitment to each other? Are you honest with each other? When you have disagreements, do you deal with them openly and in fair terms? Does each of you sacrifice for the other? When there are conflicts between you, does the same person always win and the other always lose? If the husband always loses, what does that say to little boys in the family about growing up to be a man? Or if the husband always wins, what does that say? What does it say to the little girls in the family if the wife always wins or loses?

To see how you function as parents, you need to study yourselves as a pair, a couple, parents, mom and dad, lovers, a unit, a unity. The foundation of family health, thus prevention, is the health of individual family members, but the couple relationship is the next layer in the family structure. You need to strip away all the good and bad feelings, past and present, and examine your commitment to each other *today*. Not how you felt on your wedding day or the day the first baby was born. But *today*.

Even if you are separated or divorced (maybe especially if you're separated or divorced), you need to assess honestly and calmly how your relationship affects the rest of the family. You must take a careful, truthful look at your shared values and goals. If you are divorced or separated, your children need to know more than ever that you love and care about them and that you are still their foundation, that you share the responsibility for their well-being, that you are unified as parents even though the marriage is not intact.

Kids need to know in objective and rational terms how and why the marriage failed. Don't give your kids your side. Don't dump your continuing anger toward your spouse and the failed marriage on your child. For kids who live in the single-parent home, they must understand how it got to be that way and why it should be that way. Honesty isn't just the best policy—it's the only policy.

What is it that you set out to establish on your wedding day? Do you still feel it? Are you both pulling on the same rope to get you and your family through life? Or do you often see your spouse across the mud-pit pulling on the opposite end of the rope?

You need to create a sound and secure environment for your children. Do you feel confident that because of the strong, united front the two of you as a couple have demonstrated every day, your kids have strong feelings of self-worth, and can fight any temptation or threat out there and survive it? If not, why not? Do your children know that at home their parents are united, caring and loving and ready to do whatever it takes to keep their children safe and happy? Kids' perception of parents is that they are one, two people in this life *together*. If that perception is threatened, kids get fearful, confused, distressed and disillusioned.

Does each of you pull your child in opposite directions? Do you really know each other? Have you ever taken the time to learn how your partner feels and thinks, or why he or she reacts a certain way? Do you know why your wife cries? Or do you know why your husband loses his temper and slams doors? Do you try to understand or do you get madder when she cries? Do you throw things and yell back when he slams the door? Do your children see this and watch in disbelief while their foundation cracks before their very eyes? Are they learning from this? You bet. They're learning to be scared and confused and to wonder what's wrong with their family. A home with a cracked foundation is no safe haven for a child. The couple relationship is your child's model of human relationships, and it is from this model that he learns to relate to parents, siblings and people outside the family.

Do you still do fun things together as a couple? Do you go to movies, out to dinner, plan special events together? Or do you say you're too busy? Is romance still alive in the marriage? Or is romance something you think you're too old for? Do your children look at your relationship and know you care about and love each other?

Are you honest with each other? Come on now, *really* honest? Always? Do your children know when you tell little white lies to each other? What about big black ones? Do you expect your children to behave differently and be honest with you because you tell them to? When you have disagreements, do your children see you deal with each other in terms that are fair and rational, without violence? "Just the facts, ma'am," don't drag up everything you can find out of the past and throw it on the table now. After an argument, do you make it clear to the kids that you still love each other and that you are not harboring any anger for your partner? After a fight, do you come out hugging? If you do, your kids are probably satisfied knowing that harmony doesn't always exist. But love does.

DEALING WITH THE KIDS
"DO THEY HEAR WHAT YOU SAY?"

You have already learned in the chapter on Parent Action that one of the keys to stopping a drug problem in your family is clearly defining the boundary between parents and kids. That is, parents should be parents and kids should be kids. And never the twain should meet.

This is also an important factor in prevention. Before a drug problem rears its ugly head, you need to clarify who's in charge in the family, who sets the rules, who draws the bottom lines and why. Parents set a model of authority, privilege and power that will take charge, set limits, and protect kids from the lethal consequences of immature decisions. Once the kids have proven sufficient maturity to take their places as adults in society, they can aspire to the parental model.

In the meantime, kids should be dealt with on their own terms. They should be given kid—not adult—responsibilities. They should be talked to as the kids they are, given guidelines and consequences from a sensitive and authoritative adult. This means that you as a parent have to take the time to realize that a problem that may seem trivial to you is all-consuming in the kid world. Don't dismiss as childish or irritating anything that your kid comes to you about and asks for help with. Determine if it is a real problem in his view, not in yours.

Don't apply adult solutions to kids' problems. You need to listen to an eleven-year-old in terms of eleven-year-old problems, a fourteen-year-old in terms of fourteen-year-old problems. Your child may be worried about school or a friend who drinks, or a friend's parents getting a divorce, or his or her own sexual identity. Each problem needs a specific, thoughtful, age-oriented answer, and the answer should allow the child to make his own decision based on the guidelines you have given him. Give the child sufficient time to explain the problem and give him sufficient time to understand the guidelines you are giving him. Don't make snap decisions. And don't expect your child to come to you with his problems if you're not able to deal with his problems *in kid terms* as a fair, understanding, loving, caring parent—not a judge.

There will be times when the child should be encouraged to come up with his own solutions to his own problems, and he should face the consequences of those decisions. Positive consequences reinforce his decisions. If he makes a decision and it works for him, it becomes a learning tool to make that kind of decision again. If negative or painful consequences ensue, this, too, is a learning tool. He can alter his decision so that the next time, the solution will have positive results.

Parents serve two functions in this process. First, they must act as monitors to control the limits of a child's decision so that problem-solving truly is a learning, not destructive, experience. Secondly, parents have to become coaches who interpret consequences. They must help their children look at the results of their decisions, analyze them and come up with better decisions with acceptable consequences.

Do not hand over power, authority and privileges to children and teenagers and expect them to make wise, logical decisions. It's hard enough for adults to be wise and logical. It's no surprise that a thirteen-year-old makes immature decisions. They ARE immature. And they need your help.

Just as kids can't make adult decisions, they can't be left to flounder around looking for their own set of values. In terms of prevention, it is essential that parents give children defined family values. Family rules should reflect those values in terms of governing the life of the family within the framework of family beliefs.

Family values should be right out in the open. Do your kids really know what you think about certain issues, how you feel about the world, deal with problems? The first rule in your family should be that anybody can talk about any value or any rule. Not to understand a family value or rule or not to be able to discuss it is to suspect it, fear it, feel the need to ignore it or break it. To discuss it is to understand it.

Have a family forum. The family, the most intimate unit in society, ought to be a place that's fun. A refuge when you're hurting. A family ought to be something each member is proud to be part of. Any member should be able to come to the family with any problem, no matter how embarrassing, and receive honest feedback and healing, comforting support. Open conversation about problems and pains from family members' daily run-ins with life keeps everyone in tune with everyone else's life. This makes it easier for family members to sense any discord in another family member's life. If any individual knows that all other family members are focusing on him, supporting him and approving of him, it makes it pretty tough to go out and get in trouble. Younger members, especially, need to know that the family forum is there for them as they face the problems of growing up. The family forum is fundamental to drug prevention.

Prevention will be most likely to work when you can be honest and open with all aspects of your lives and all the lives of members of the family. It means everybody knows and understands the family values and rules. It means anybody can talk about anything within the family love circle.

Families ought to provide an atmosphere in which all family members feel valuable, worthwhile. No matter if they are short or tall, fat or thin. Each person is valued for who he or she is as an individual and what he or she brings to the family.

Families have two messages that need to be communicated to its members. The first is the accepting kind of love message we talked about. No matter who you are and what you are, you are valued and loved because you are a member of this family. The second is one of bottom lines. Depending on the family value system, certain kinds of behavior are acceptable and rewarded and other kinds of behavior are unacceptable and penalized. But applying consequences when that value system is violated does not mean that the individual is any less loved. Every member of the family needs to understand that the two family messages do not contradict each other, that in fact it is *because* the individual is valued and worthwhile that bottom lines are drawn. Bottom lines exist because parents care about their children, children care about their parents, parents care about each other and children care about each other. Bottom lines are part of the accepting love message. If a bottom line is violated, the security of the family atmosphere is threatened.

Every member of a family has to be encouraged to grow as an individual, in keeping with the accepting love message. There are times when a family member may want to grow in a direction that will require the support, even sacrifice, of other family members. For example, if Mom decides to go back to school, everybody else in the family may have to pitch in to help with household jobs. Or if Suzie decides to go on to medical school, Johnny may have to agree to go to a less expensive school to help with the family's education fund. It is this kind of backing of each other and each other's growth that ties people together. Families become families not because they all live under the same roof but because they contribute to each other's well-being.

The final area of prevention is to have a family that *does* things together. Not a family that shares only a last name, an address, and a laundry room. Not a family that eats at separate times, each member going his or her separate way. Don't let the hectic schedule of two working parents and children involved in various activities stop your family from having a designated family time. Because ours is a mobile, multimedia society, teenagers find ways to avoid being part of the family. By the time children reach twelve or thirteen years old, they no longer think it's cool to be seen with their parents or a brother or sister. The child's withdrawal from the family is usually attributed to "that strange period kids go through." Daughters no longer want to go shopping with their mothers. Sons don't want to be hugged after the winning game. Or kissed when they are heading off on the class trip. Teenagers often do not even want to share meals with the rest of the family. They'd prefer to eat in their rooms, in front of the television, at a friend's house or just say that they're not hungry. These are all signs of a weakening of the family ties. How does a parent regain those ties with a teenager and not lose them with younger children?

First of all, it is the parents' responsibility to insist upon family activities. Again, this is a bottom line. It is not something about which children have any say. There will be certain meals that the family has together, no matter what the dance classes, baseball practice or social schedules demand. For example, Sunday night can be family night. It might be a night for popcorn and television after dinner. It may be a night that the family sees a movie together. Or it may be the night chosen for family forum. In any case, parents need to designate some mealtimes, some evenings, some activities that keep the family operating as a family. Attending church or synagogue or visiting grandparents should not be events that children are allowed to give up when they become teenagers. They must remain family activities.

Some people suggest that making demands on teenagers only reinforces their stubborn rebellion. The fact is, all teenagers test the adult world's limits and expectations. It's a normal part of the growing up process. The kids who find no boundaries, as a rule, become very distressed and disturbed in their development. Teenagers feel most comfortable when, as they test family boundaries, they find secure limits and expectations. They find that their parents care enough to say, "You really belong." Often when a parent has been too permissive and suddenly changes the game, it takes time for the teenager to accept the change and become comfortable. That's okay. It's worth the effort.

To encourage a teenager's willingness to join in family activities, use your dinner discussions or another family gathering to have each family member suggest what he might like the family to do together. Perhaps a teenager would like his family to take skiing lessons together. Of if the child has some special interest in a subject, he might like the family vacation to include a stop at a museum or Dodger Stadium or a ride on a steamboat down the Mississippi. There are things close to home that a teenager might be pleased to have his family join him in, even though it may take some coaxing. A swimming meet, an antique car show, a dirt-bike race—most teenagers just won't volunteer to invite their parents unless they are encouraged.

Sometimes the family should do things alone; other times, family members should be allowed to bring along friends. The more pride a teenager takes in his family, the less likely he is to violate the family's value systems. Getting together with other families will give the child a wider field in which to experience his self-worth, acceptance and value as a human being. Including other generations of the family also gives the child a larger foundation of people who feel good about him. Older family generations, grandparents, aunts, uncles, reinforce the family system as a strong, ongoing, determining structure. The activities a family shares should be balanced by each member's *individual* activities. Dad may belong to a service club. Mom may volunteer at the hospital twice a week. A daughter could enjoy gymnastics or a son might love baseball. Members can support each other through their individual activities and then join together in family activities.

If your family is drug free, put prevention practices to work at once. If you see a cloud on the horizon, reach out for your kids as you've never reached out before. Reach inside yourself as you've never reached. And reach inside your family and touch every member with loving, caring honesty.

Instill in your kids the idea that life is learning about themselves and the world. It's about setting goals and feeling good about themselves without any need for chemicals. Encourage them when they do well. Redirect them when they get confused and make mistakes. And find them when they get lost and reset their compasses. Use compassion and firmness. Prevention is the easiest step to take in the drug war. And the most valuable.

Prevention Checklist

1. Do you find it easier to be absorbed with your children's activities and problems than to look at life and deal with your own needs and feelings?
2. Is there an alcoholic or drug abuser among your parents, grandparents or other close relatives?
3. Do you push your son to play football because your father pushed you? Are the activities you share with your children the same as those your parents did with you?
4. Are you pushing your daughter to date early because you didn't have much of a social life in high school? Are you permissive with your son because your father was so strict with you?
5. Are you so obsessed with work that you neglect exercise and fun?
6. Are you so concerned with taking care of your home and children that you don't do social things with friends?
7. Do you have an open and supportive relationship with your spouse?
8. Are you an "in-charge" parent or are you a "buddy" to your children?
9. Do you feel under pressure at times? Do you feel blue, low and depressed too much? Do you know why?
10. Do you know what's really going on with your kids? What they are afraid of? What's going right? What isn't going right? What they would really like for their lives right now?
11. What are your family's beliefs and values about God, spirituality, morals, the meaning of life, sex, family and so on? Do you talk openly about them? Is the family's belief and value system a cohesive one? Do all family members understand it?
12. Do your children see you practice your values? Are your children learning by what you tell them or what you show them in your day-to-day living?
13. Does your family share in regular activities together? How many meals do you have together? Do you share in talk?

What do you do together for fun? Does everybody partici-
pate in special activities for other family members?

14. *When your family is together, do you attend to important*
    family business? Are your children afraid to talk about
    their problems with other family members?
15. *Do you feel valued, cared about and important when you*
    are with the family? Does your spouse? Do each of your
    children? Do you and does every member of the family
    work to make every other family member feel valuable and
    worthwhile?

9

The Healthy Family
"Building strong bodies . . . and minds . . . and souls . . . and . . ."

Most Americans have a fantasy picture of the perfect family, based on everything from the way grandma did it to what they see in cornflake commercials. Is the healthy family the one that has breakfast together every morning? The one that takes vitamins daily? The one that goes to church or synagogue every week? Or the one that has 2.5 children?

The healthy family has nothing to do with having a station wagon, a dog, a white picket fence or a riding lawnmower. It has nothing to do with camping trips or window boxes planted with geraniums. Healthy families are not the families found in television shows or movies. Family life isn't like all those television situation comedies in which problems are resolved in thirty minutes.

The profile of the American family is changing. Today, only seventy-five percent of kids under eighteen years old still live

208

with both parents. And when the going gets tough at home, there are no cuts to commercials. So modeling family life on "Ozzie and Harriet" and the boys is unrealistic. It makes it difficult for people to believe in their own families. And in real life, where people live together twenty-four hours a day, seven days a week, the grinding conflicts between parent and child, between siblings, between husband and wife, add up to a picture that is less than television fantasy.

Real fathers aren't Robert Young. Real mothers aren't Donna Reed. And real kids aren't the Mouseketeers. But that doesn't mean the family is second-rate or that family members are mediocre.

WHAT IS A FAMILY?

"IT'S AN OLD FAMILY RECIPE."

"Together" is the operational word in a family. Each family is a unique mixture of happy and warm and wonderful things, of sad and painful and tragic events, but all things they experienced together. So that even when a family is not physically joined together under the same roof, a healthy family is together spiritually, mentally and emotionally—in both sad and happy times.

A family is a magical event in the affairs of man—it's an event because families happen, they don't merely exist. And it happens continuously. It expands to accommodate growth and movement. It contracts and toughens to ward off whatever outside forces attack the family.

But while a healthy family is a living, wondrous thing, it is an entity that takes a great deal of time and work and love. It takes constant, honest communication. It takes rules and regulations. It has to be flexible enough to permit change but stable enough always to be a safe harbor.

FAMILY PROBLEMS
"DEALING WITH THE WARTS."

Real families—even the healthiest, happiest ones—have problems. That's a fact of life. Problems are inescapable—problems about kids growing up, problems with couples trying to work out a lifetime of love and marriage while people's needs are changing, problems with people's internal clocks not always being synchronized, problems with different likes and dislikes.

At times there are major problems, like a serious illness, economic problems, loss of a job or a major disappointment for a kid in terms of school, sports or career. There are also natural losses in life. Kids grow up and move away from home. People lose their natural youthful appearance, flat tummies give way to bulges, peaches 'n' cream complexions get wrinkles. Lifetime dreams are sacrificed for new, more realistic dreams. The death of a friend. Or the death of a family member, maybe even an immediate family member. With death comes a sense of pain and loss. And when death involves the parent generation, there is also a sense of change.

Real families have warts *and* beauty spots, triumphs *and* disasters.

It is the "how" of dealing with problems that indicates whether a family is healthy or not. Healthy families deal with problems, all problems, in a constructive and growing way. Unhealthy families tend to be scarred or fundamentally changed by both the minor difficulties and the major traumas. Healthy families reaffirm their self-worth, their skills and talents, their entire process as a family by how they handle the minor difficulties and the major disasters.

How do healthy families handle the minor everyday "warts"? A healthy family turns a problem into an opportunity. The family unit helps the child and the adult turn depression, fear and anxiety into a sense of hope. For example, a conflict develops between Susie and Bobby over a certain toy. An unhealthy parent would resolve the issue by decree in order to get the immediate irritation to go away. "Bobby, you get the puzzle. Susie, you get the book. I don't want to hear any more about it. You heard what I said." The problem may have been resolved but nobody in the family has learned anything from the conflict. In this kind of family, the answer to "why" is "because I said so." In a healthy family, "whys" have real answers with solid reasoning.

A parent in a healthy family would use the conflict between Susie and Bobby over the toy to sit down and help the kids find their own solution to the problem. So, instead of having an adult-controlled situation, it would become a learning experience for the two kids about how to deal cooperatively in a family.

Another example: Every afternoon Johnny comes home from school scruffed up and every morning he doesn't want to go back. The parent figures that some kids are picking on him, beating him up on the playground. In the unhealthy family, the father would mutter unpleasant words about "those little punks" and tell Johnny to go to school and "beat the crap out of 'em. Give 'em a dose of their own medicine." In the healthy family, the parents would try to work out with the child what it was that was causing the playground fights and then help the child resolve the problem himself. Because Johnny is likely to encounter this or a similar problem again, Johnny needs to make his own decision and solve his own problem. Parents should serve as resources. This not only allows him to deal with the immediate situation but it prepares him for future problem-solving.

Even a minor problem can be an opportunity to grow and learn and take responsibility. It is not only a good technique for child development, it is a good technique for healthy family growth. Treating each minor problem as an opportunity for learning and growing enhances the whole process of being a family.

Major problems like death, financial stress or a family member in trouble are harder to handle for the family. Often, major disasters bring with them panicky, frightened and anxious responses. Out of the trauma, catastrophe and anxiety, healthy families begin to sort out what can be done using the family's resources to address the problem.

When a disaster hits, a healthy family tends to pull together. Family members drop nonessential activities to become a team in support of the person with the problem. A closeness develops, a sense of support, and above all, individual sacrifice for the sake of the individual in trouble.

Secondly, the family dealing with a major disaster does not use dishonesty to make the problem go away. Nor do they explain it away. Most people have a tendency when they are in trouble to blame someone else, rather than to look at the situation realistically. In healthy families, while one individual or another may start to engage in blaming, rationalizing or shaking fists at the gods, other members help correct the rationalization and bring everyone back to the real, cold facts of the situation. After all, you cannot bring the family resources to bear, you cannot move from problem to solution unless you are dealing with the real facts.

Using reality and honesty, the family conveys a strong sense of love and support. The person who is under the stress is not allowed to feel, be or act worthless because the family message says, "Hey, you're still our brother . . . sister, father, mother, husband, wife . . . you're still loved and worthwhile in spite of the immediate situation. It is the situation itself that we're having to cope with. It's not you as a person." That fundamental message of self-worth with the real facts makes it possible to then move on and use the talents of the family to find the solution.

As the family rides out the tidal waves of feelings, family members can start to work toward solutions. They do not solve the problem for the person in trouble because that would undermine that person's self-worth and sense of dignity. What the family members do is to make sure the responsibility rests on the person with the problem, but help with ideas, questions and what they can contribute as a team to help the person solve the problem. The person with the problem has to take the initiative in solving the difficulty in order to come out of it with a sense of being his own master, being able to solve his own problems and having a sense of self-worth.

As the person with the problem assumes responsibility, the family forum becomes a think tank for ideas. Even the smallest child may naively ask a question or come up with a solution to the problem. The family encourages the individual to take action to solve the problem. After all, the victim of the disaster can be just that: a helpless, hopeless victim. Or he can be someone with a problem who is going to take responsibility and do something about it. Encouragement to take action is an important step in the process.

Once a plan is formulated and a decision is made, things start to coalesce towards a solution and the resources of the entire family come into play. A wife can go back to work to help with the financial solution. Dad can share the responsibility in the house to free Mother to go back to work. Kids can contribute to the needs of the family. This way, everyone has a sense of pride: "We took our problem and we solved it and we all helped."

And finally, there is the business of how you turn the problem into a piece of family history. Unhealthy families tend to stigmatize the person with the problem forever—whether it is solved or not. The cousin who got pregnant. The uncle who used to have a drinking problem. They almost literally have the problem branded across their foreheads. The person is never allowed to outlive who they were in terms of their problem.

In a healthy family, the problem and its solution are converted into family history. They become major benchmarks in which the qualities of the person are demonstrated and validated, but in which the person is separate and different from the event. In other words, "You're not the problem. You're a person who had a problem and, with the help of a family, triumphed over it." That kind of family history, that kind of interpretation after the fact is important in keeping people individuals and in maintaining the family as a living process. People are not warts. People have warts. They come and they go. But the individual is still the person with the shining face, the special qualities, the love and the care.

So, instead of derailing the healthy family, minor difficulties and major disasters become the basis for satisfaction, pride and growth. The family's strength in the face of problems is a good test of health and well-being as a unit. It's an attitude. It's how you see the normal difficulties of life and how you see the major problems. It's how you see change. It's the thoughts you have about your family and its ability to solve problems. It's how you look at problems themselves. Do they appear solvable or insurmountable? Do they look like hurdles or obstacle courses? All of these set you up to grow and move ahead. And the ability to grow and move ahead enhances each person's sense of self.

REAL OR ROLE?

"HEY, IT'S REALLY ME."

As we've seen, unhealthy families turn to role-playing to survive chemical dependency. But healthy families are different. They are made up of individuals, not people protecting themselves with made-up roles. Family members are seen in totality, a rich, complex totality.

When unhealthy family members assume roles, they become caricatures. Predictable caricatures. In order to survive, they respond to the same problem the same way time after time after time. If A, then B. It doesn't take long for others to determine the stereotyped behavior of each role-player. The result is that pretty soon every family member knows the parts that others play, their actions and their responses, and life becomes a rote experience.

The other danger is that individuals begin to see themselves the way others see them. They lock themselves inside their new roles so tightly that they lose all touch with their natural identity. But whether it is how others see you or how you see yourself, people become robots when they adopt roles. And robots have no feelings. So the defensive behavior that protects an individual from pain and hurt also prevents him from experiencing joy and happiness. And it takes both pain and joy to be a full human being.

In healthy families, there are only two roles and those have to do with how a person functions in the family. The first role is that of the parent—mature, responsible, caring, supportive— a person who sets limits and who makes the world safe for the persons in the other role, kids. The role of the child is to be himself and to grow and to learn about himself in a framework of respect for family members and curiosity about life and the world.

Those are healthy roles. But the roles themselves never get in the way of being an individual. In other words, people aren't just parents or just kids. They are individuals with childhoods, histories, special interests, different ways of smiling or frowning, funny habits, all the things that make them people, separate from their role. Mom isn't just a parent. She's a woman. She sings in the choir at church. She's a real estate agent. She likes to garden. She's a good cook. She hates housecleaning but does it anyway. She reads a lot. And she's allergic to peanuts. Matt isn't just a kid either. He's a second-grader. He doesn't like vegetables. He can rollerskate. He saw *E.T.* twice and cried both times. He makes noises like a truck. He's a little shy and very loving. And he knows more than you'd ever want to know about dinosaurs.

Healthy people let you know who they really are. They expose their inner thoughts and feelings by everything they do and say. That doesn't mean that healthy people "spill their guts" all the time. Rather, it means the real part of who they are comes shining through. What they say and how they behave are authentic expressions of who they really are.

Healthy people expose their inside feelings through outside actions. Healthy families produce people who are open and expressive. And healthy families encourage others to express themselves in an honest and individual way, too.

Differences are accepted, even applauded, in the healthy family. Just because John is the first redhead in the family in four generations doesn't mean he's an outsider. It means he has something special about him. There are no cookie cutters marked "Smith" or "Jones" or "Wilson" to turn out people. Families are the people-making process.

Healthy families help each other deal with the peer pressure and the social pressure outside the family. Kids, particularly, face pressures from teachers who want them to be good students, coaches who want them to be good athletes, Sunday school or synagogue teachers who have certain expectations, friends who want them to join in the fun and so on. There are role models at home, in the community, in sports, on television, in the movies. All of which creates pressure to conform. Parents and brothers and sisters need to understand the outside pressures in order to encourage each kid to "be yourself."

Families don't have to be all-American to be healthy. Dad can be out of work. He can be the guy who worries about the mortgage but also the guy who goes into every kid's room to say good night. The guy who has to take medicine daily for his high blood pressure and the guy who misses life in Omaha, where he grew up.

Mom can be a single parent. She may not get home from work until 6:00 P.M. So she defrosts more than she cooks. She doesn't know anything about cars and always gets taken to the cleaners by car mechanics. When it was her turn to take cupcakes to the PTA committee meeting, she forgot. She loves Oriental flower arranging. And she flunked her first try at the real estate exam so she's really working hard to pass it the next time around.

Healthy does not mean being perfect. Healthy means being real, no matter where life finds you. In an apartment or a mansion. Working or staying at home. Young or old. Climbing the ladder or at the top. Healthy can exist in any family.

Communication in the healthy family is not tuning out because you think you know what another person has to say. Healthy families expect differences, surprises and freshness in their interactions. There is a curiosity about each person, what went on in their day and what's going on in their lives. Each day adds to the history of a person.

Gift-giving is one good thermometer of the healthy family. Do the people in your family give gifts that recognize caring for each other's interests or do they give gifts that have nothing to do with the individual? Did somebody give Dad a necktie for his birthday when he's known for his crazy love of bowties? Did somebody give Tommy a Dallas Cowboys jersey when his favorite team is the Washington Redskins? Or did someone give Mom a book on English cottages because they know how much she loves English architecture? Did someone give Molly a real poster from the Joffrey Ballet tour to encourage her love of dance? If gifts for birthdays, Christmas and other special occasions are routine, obligatory kinds of gifts, it's a pretty safe bet people are doing more role-reacting than really interacting. A family that cherishes every member as a human being has a lot of fun selecting the "perfect gift." There is an element of humor and warmth associated with gift-giving when there is love and care given to finding appropriate and meaningful presents.

You can also determine the health of your family by looking at your daily lifestyle. Is it dead, dull and dry? Do Mom and Dad do the same thing every day when they get home from work? Do the kids do the same thing every day when they get home from school? Is dinner a routine and not a family gathering? Do people walk through the paces of living together or do they really live together? Do family members watch the same TV shows all the time or is there conflict about who wants to see what? Conflict is not necessarily bad. There is healthy conflict too. People want to do different things at different times and feel different ways about different events. Families in which people are real and not playing roles have healthy conflict because individuals within the family grow and change.

Life without healthy conflict is boring, monotonous and uninspiring. Angry conflict is debilitating. Healthy conflict is rejuvenating.

SEXUAL ROLES
KEN OR BARBIE?

The trend of the women's movement in the last couple of decades has been to treat people as individuals, regardless of sex. And that's good. But sexual identity is a fundamental part of the personality. What it means to be male or female is a physically and culturally determined issue. But it's not only how other people see you. It's how you see yourself.

Both parents and kids have sexual roles and those roles need to be worked out in healthy ways. Sexual identities should not overcome or obscure individual identity. For example, just because Amy is a female, it does not mean that she has to like dolls more than sports or literature or science. Sexual identity should not keep Tony from liking poetry and dance class. Just because he's male doesn't mean he has to be a lineman on the football team.

Part of what goes on between parents and their children is sex role-modeling, what it means in that family to be male or female. Kids learn by copying. Puberty, especially, brings with it a self-consciousness about sex and sexuality. Being a particular sex includes the way you communicate, how you dress, your body language, how you relate to people of the same sex and how you relate to members of the opposite sex. Healthy families produce people who are comfortable with people of their own sex and with people of the opposite sex. And most of all, the healthy family produces people who are comfortable with their own sexuality. The relationship a child has with the parent of the same sex and the interaction he has with the parent of the opposite sex are his models for sexual identity.

FAMILY TRADITIONS
"HISTORY IN THE MAKING."

Every family has traditions, whether it's the kind of ornament on top of the Christmas tree or a religious celebration. Families are made up of generations of traditions, some of which are stringently observed and others of which are modified as they get passed on from generation to generation.

Tradition is an important part of the healthy family. Society's traditions and the family's own personal traditions provide the child with a foundation upon which to grow and change. Traditions give a family stability. They provide texture, depth and lots of tools for daily living. It would be impossible for parents to create "from scratch" all the ingredients necessary for a strong family. Parents have to draw on their family histories in order to weave their own family fabric.

Traditions have to do with religious beliefs, moral values, where people come from, ethnic background and rituals for special occasions and holidays. Traditions help weave the pattern in a family's life fabric. Without tradition, a family can be sterile, placid, vacant and empty.

What about the traditions in your family that have to do with your parents and your parents' parents? Do you talk about them as a family and the value they bring because of the people with whom they are associated? Do you have traditions in your home that have to do with family occasions in other towns, other states or other countries? Are there traditions in your family that your kids take pride in and like to share with other kids who have different traditions? Those particular pieces of the rich family fabric that are intergenerational are a major part of a child's sense of stability and structure. It's something that "belongs" to the child and to the family. Whether it's the Italian immigrant's family that serves pasta with the Christmas turkey or the midwestern family reunion, the Irish celebration of St. Patrick's Day, the Jewish seder, the Catholic observance of Lent or southerners getting together to crank the ice cream freezer and make homemade ice cream. . . . It's all tradition.

The problem with tradition, of course, is that it can become a straitjacket. If it is treated as something that always has been and always will be, it becomes harsh and severe. Children need to be able to question and to understand traditions. Traditions that are explained with colorful family stories become rich, warm and loving. Traditions that are expected to be observed and honored just because "that's the way it's always been" become rigid and binding.

So flexibility has to go hand in hand with tradition. Traditions should not get in the way of kids functioning with other kids. They should not interfere with the interaction between parent and child. Flexibility does not mean throwing away or ignoring the rich and valuable past of a family. It simply means that traditions should respond to the needs of the present generation. Flexibility means having the freedom from the past to choose who you are going to be today and where you are going tomorrow. For example, for generations Paul's family had worked in the steel mills. His family had always had blue-collar jobs. His family was also devoutly Catholic. His grandfather had moved to the United States as a young man from southern Italy and the family still had big Italian dinners every Sunday. When Paul finished high school, he got a scholarship to college. He was the first person in his family to go to college. He wanted to be a writer. Grandpa was proud that his grandson didn't work in the mills anymore but he wasn't so glad to see him go off to live in New York City. Paul got his master's degree and became quite successful as a free-lance writer. For a long time, he didn't understand just how valuable a part of his life tradition was. He had forgotten a lot about the old neighborhood, the two-story shingled house, the smell of the steel mills. But he hadn't forgotten his grandfather's stories about southern Italy, "the old country." He hadn't forgotten Sunday dinner. And he still never missed midnight mass on Christmas Eve. Not until Paul had children of his own did he understand the part tradition had played in his life. He wanted to pass on that same warmth, that sense of belonging to something special, to his own children. But he also wanted to give them the flexibility that his family had given him, the freedom to leave the blue-collar life that had served his family for generations, in search of something new, a new kind of belonging.

Flexibility is the ability to choose between the tradition, the heritage of the family, and the invention of new ways, new thoughts and new techniques for coping with life. It permits people to adapt to new situations and to accommodate their own needs.

Parents can best encourage flexibility in the healthy family by sharing with their children the traditions they have chosen to preserve. They should help their children understand them and, at the same time, help them find new ways to do new things. Parents should instill an attitude in their children that the past is precious and worth preserving but the future is exciting and worth exploring. Children should also understand that tradition is a tool for understanding the future. By combining family traditions with what they learn today, they can create their own traditions.

THE SUPPORT SYSTEM
"GETTING THE MINIMUM DAILY REQUIREMENTS."

Traditionally, the family has been the basic unit of support for meeting human needs.

In most societies, it is the family that teaches a child language skills, social skills, sexual behavior and even a trade. Little girls learn how to be wives and mothers. Little boys learn to be husbands, fathers, breadwinners. And families pass on occupational skills from generation to generation. Older family members teach the young. Age is revered for its experience and wisdom.

But in American society, the family is no longer the main support system. In many respects it has been replaced by a series of outside institutions. Day-care centers and Head Start programs are supposed to nurture but instead preempt the fam-

ily nurturing system. The public schools are supposed to edu-
cate young children. The medical system is supposed to care
for the sick. The mental health system is supposed to help
people deal with the stress and distress in their lives. Voca-
tional schools teach people trades. All in all, there is a larger
range of outside influences on the individual. And those influences have taken away much of the family's role.

But is it working? Is the "new, improved, Americanized"
family better off? It would appear not. The suicide rate is increasing. The demand for mental health care is increasing. The
number of alcohol and drug dependency cases is increasing. It
would appear that when families stopped being the basic, primary unit of support, the system failed. Institutions cannot
fulfill human needs as well as the family. The traditional family
takes care of the smallest child and the eldest grandparent and
each person has his own part to play in the "cradle-to-the-
grave" process.

The American family unit is constantly under assault. The
divorce rate assaults the family. Modern mobility assaults the
family. And even television, video games and cable networks
assault the family by distracting people from real, basic communication.

Today's family in America has to work particularly hard at
surviving those assaults and providing a strong support system. The healthy family has to provide a small child with all
of the sustenance necessary to live and grow. As people get
older, the family has to remain the basic system of support for
dealing with the problems of life. Even adults need to return
continually to the "family well." A person never outgrows his
need for the family support system. And the family has to be
the intimate group with which a person can celebrate successes in a way that one could never do with a stranger. A
family not only has to allow people to grow, it has to encourage
people to reach their maximum potential. The family should be
a place where a person feels free to test new ideas, new goals,
new personality traits and the need for change. The family
should be a familiar and intimate place where the most impor-

tant moments of one's life are shared.

If a family is to provide a strong support system, it also has to be a place of struggle and conflict. A place where family members can become who they are and dream about who they will be through problem and solution, through tradition and flexibility. A person struggling with those conflicts needs the honest feedback of people bound by blood and family bond. Family love and support make it possible for a person to be rooted while struggling to grow.

The needs of individuals within the family change rather dramatically during a lifetime. Changes are affected by biological growth as one moves from being small and dependent to being large and independent. It changes as the romantic love of a young couple matures into a life together and parenting. Then again as children leave the nest. Then again as a couple deals with the disappointments of middle age and the limitations of the aging process itself. Dimensions of need change with age—the need for privacy versus supervision, space versus closeness. There are needs of the spirit and social needs. And there are changing physical health needs. So the family support system has to change to accommodate change.

Occasionally, the family has to sit down and assess where it is, how it is handling people's changes and how it is functioning as a support system. Each individual has to think about his own needs and if they are being met. If you have teenagers, are you still operating your family support system as if they were small children? Is your family support system appropriate to where people are in their own growth and aging cycles? Is the support in your family only physical support—food, clothing and shelter? Or is the system providing emotional, social and spiritual support as well? Are each and every family member's needs being met?

The healthy family is not healthy just because someone is bringing home the bacon. Emotional needs can only be met if physical needs are met but physical needs themselves are not enough. In a number of studies about support systems done with animals, baby animals growing up in isolation, rather than with the support of a parent, have usually died before reaching adulthood.

The family is the most reliable and only really successful support system. Unlike any other institution, the family can underscore learning with love and can accentuate teaching with touching and understanding.

PEOPLE-MAKING

"READY, AIM, FIRE."

Families are not factories. There is no manufacturing process that stamps out new products identical to the previous ones. It is more like the work of a craftsman who takes a raw product and turns it into something rare, and it is the interaction between the artisan and the material that determines the quality of the work. So it is with people-making. It is the interaction between parents and children that determines the quality of the family.

Most parents approach the task of people-making without any training or skill. There's some sort of unquestioned belief that a person is born with either motherly or fatherly instincts, that because a person is born with either female or male equipment, gets married and can biologically reproduce, that that same person is equipped for the business of people-making. Wrong. It's not so simple.

When "the two of us" becomes the "three of us," it is no time to shoot from the hip. Being a parent requires careful marksmanship in order to hit the target—a healthy family.

Before a couple even starts to consider having a baby, they should stop and think about turning their "couple thinking" into "family thinkings." And are they able to do it? The two o'clock feedings and the terrible twos are the least of their worries. They've probably done some readjusting already to become a couple. They came into the marriage as two independent human beings. It took some matter of adjusting just to figure out who got what closet and whose favorite piece of art was going to get the honored spot over the couch. Those decisions didn't come easily. Then it grew into whose church they would attend and how they would divide the household responsibilities. Who takes charge of the checkbook and pays the monthly bills. And which family to spend Christmas or other special holidays with. It's not easy. Give a little here, take a little there and you've got a couple. It becomes a two-way street. Add a baby, one baby, then maybe another, and the two-way street becomes a traffic circle. That traffic circle is a real family. It keeps on going, sharing family history, learning family traditions and then going on to leave its own history and traditions. The decision to be a parent adds another limb to your family tree. Once a couple has children, they automatically contribute to the next generation of the family history. It's awesome. But most people deciding to have children don't think about any of this. Instead, they wonder: Who does the baby look like? Can we afford to have a child? Will it help or hurt our marriage? Does it mean giving up our freedom? Most people never got as far as thinking what it is about themselves and their family history and traditions they want to give away to future generations.

Unlike the couple situation, which is (optimistically) give and take, becoming a parent is a give and give proposition. Babies can't give back. They depend on the parents to give to them. Their mere survival depends on the parents' giving. Oh sure, babies give warm, good, serene feelings to parents but they don't physically give back. So what you've learned as an adult—the "give-and-get" school of living—doesn't apply. So the first decision a would-be healthy parent has to make is that he or she is willing to give to someone who can't give back yet.

Then the couple has to consider: What is it that we are as a couple? What is it about our couple relationship that we want to pass on? What can we give to a child, the torchbearer of our families' future generations? Most adults have a hard time thinking of themselves as a part of history. It's difficult to see beyond the now of chores, traffic jams, job challenges and personal responsibilities to where you're going. But where you're going is as important as where you are and where you've been.

In parenting, there's no such thing as going out of business. You can't give up your lease or sell your option. Once you're in the business of people-making, you're in it for keeps. There's no turning back. The business of new life in a family never stops. Children become adults who have children who become adults and so on. A family is a growing, living organic process.

One of the ways of determining what it is that your children are learning from you about people-making is to watch them play house. Does your little girl talk lovingly to her dolls, cuddle them and support them? Or does she yell at them, get impatient and shake her finger in their little rubber faces? Does your little boy show loving feelings when he plays "family" with other children? Or does he order everybody around? How they play and how they act out in a pretend family is a simplification and exaggeration of how they see their own families—essentially, a mirror of your people-making behavior.

There is no right way and no wrong way to people-making. Each parent and each family devises its own process. There are no formulas. No blueprints. But people-making does take careful thought, vision and planning. Because remember, a piece of art can be no better than the relationship between the artist and the raw material.

HUG THERAPY

"REACH OUT, REACH OUT AND TOUCH SOMEONE."

Those telephone ads, "Reach out, reach out and touch someone," have more to offer than just telephone rings. They have a ring of reality, a ring of truth. They offer good sound advice.

No one of any age ever outgrows the need to be touched. It starts in the womb and goes to the deathbed. The first communication a child receives is inside the womb, through the skin.

Once an infant is born, he still needs that sense of touch. Before a child can see or smell or control movement, he gets warm feelings from being close. It's the most primary level of communication, and no matter how complicated life gets, no matter how successful a person becomes, no matter how far geographically or psychologically a person may wander, she or he never outgrows that need to be touched.

There is a T-shirt on the market that shows two bears embracing each other in a big "bear" hug. There are all kinds of little marks sparking from their bodies to indicate good feelings, the kind of marks cartoonists use to tell you something exciting is going on. Across the shirt, it reads "Hug Therapist." Well, hug therapy, bear hugs and all, is important to healthy families. It is as necessary for the moments of pain and family anguish as it is for the moments of joy and celebration. Hug therapy works.

HOW IT FEELS

"AM I HEALTHY YET?"

The real question is how the healthy family feels overall. Through the ups and downs, the good and bad, through the pain and pleasure, the tragedies and triumphs, how does it really feel to be part of your family?

Being a part of a family ought to feel stable and solid. No matter where you have traveled, or where you have gone, or how old you have become, the family that you return to has the kind of stability and soundness that regenerates your batteries, your creativity and your energy for life.

The family ought to feel good. Even with the arguments and all the other pressures, the family should have a kind of warmth that says you are loved, that it feels good to be here and that you are cared for. The healthy family feels energetic. There is a kind of excitement that encourages people to go ahead and do the things they want to do. The feeling of energy is a feeling of life because life itself feels good in the healthy family.

The healthy family challenges people to be their best. Interaction with your family causes you to stretch your imagination, to stretch your talents, to use your discipline and become what you want to be.

The family should be a place where people touch each other, where hugging reaffirms the love family members have for one another. The healthy family does things together, shares family chores, takes an interest in the activities of others and shares planned time with each other.

Finally, the healthy family is contagious. It makes you want to do it again because of what you have gotten. Because of how it feels to be part of a family, you have an overwhelming desire to recreate the best of that family again with your own mate and your own children. And so the business of people-making and nurturing, the business of relating to people in the intimacy of a family goes on forever because you caught it from your own family.

The healthy family feels good. Pass it on.

The Healthy Family Checklist:

1. How do you show your commitment to your family? How does your spouse show you that you and the family are important? How do your children express their trust in the family as a haven and home base?
2. Are mother and daughters expected to be alike? Do girls only do "feminine" things? Are the boys expected to be like Dad? Are the males all macho? Can people break the molds and be who they want to be inside the family?
3. Is it okay to make a mistake in your family? Are you held responsible or do you get away with it? Do the other family members ignore it or give you support while you clean it up and make changes?
4. How does it feel to be part of your family? Does it feel warm, strong, dependable, fun? Does it at times feel just comfortable and other times really exciting?
5. What traditions are an important part of your family life-style? Are they etched in stone and unquestionable or can you talk about them and improve them?
6. Are parents parents and are kids kids in your family?
7. Do you have a support system that works in your family? When somebody is in trouble or just needs advice, does the family work for them? When you have a problem do you find yourself saying, "I'm gonna go home for help," or do you feel the need to keep it from the family?
8. Are family members playing roles or are they real?
9. How much thought goes into the kind of gifts you give each other?
10. Do you have plans, real plans, to help turn your children into adults or do you ad-lib people-making?
11. Is your family a place where it feels safe to be?
12. Is hugging and touching common in your house?
13. Do family members encourage each other to be what they want to be or do family members use the words ought, should and must when dealing with other family members' aspirations?

14. *Do your children play house in happy, healthy ways? Do your kids act out rigid, harsh relationships? Does their pretend family have stereotyped male and female roles or do they play family in warm, good-feeling, pleasant ways?*
15. *Will they feel so good about their healthy family that they will want to make a healthy family for themselves?*

Kid's Drug Slang Glossary

angel dust: phencyclidine, which is a disassociative drug used as an animal tranquilizer; it causes hallucinations and comes in powder form.

bag: also called "baggie"; refers to an amount of marijuana in a plastic bag that may vary in size and cost.

be cool: a slang term that encourages one to conform to and remain in the drug-use lifestyle.

biscuit: a slang term for a Quaalude, which is methaqualone—a nonbarbiturate hypnotic-sedative drug; it is a central nervous system depressant, that is, a "down"; it is usually found in pill form.

black beauties: a type of amphetamine, that is, "speed"; it is a central nervous system stimulant that causes an aroused, excited state.

blasted: an extremely "high" or intoxicated state.

blow some dope: smoking marijuana.

bong:
a device for smoking marijuana modeled on the water pipe, it supposedly intensifies the intoxicating effect of marijuana and allegedly reduces some of the harmful by-products.

bong hit:
a single inhalation of marijuana smoke from a bong.

bowl:
the part of a pipe that holds the marijuana; also the amount of marijuana required to fill a pipe or bong.

brew:
a slang term for a can or bottle of beer.

bummer:
a bad experience with a drug high; also it is used to refer to all kinds of negative experiences.

burned out:
a physical and psychological state during which the user is coming down from the high and feels "wasted" and washed out.

burn-out:
a user who is high or intoxicated all the time; characterized by a dull, drugged look;

busted:
once used to refer to being caught at drug use or related activities by the police, this term has also come to refer to apprehension by parents, school officials, or other adults.

buzzed:
a slang term for being high on alcohol, marijuana, or any other drug.

'caine:
a slang term for cocaine, a strong central nervous system stimulant (an "up"), which most often comes in white powdered form.

carburetor:
a marijuana pipe with an extra hole for increasing the impact of inhalation: (See shotgun)

Christmas trees:
amphetamines, or "speed," central nervous system stimulants that produce an aroused, excited state.

crystal meth:
methedrine or desoxyn; a soluble amphetamine that comes in white crystal form and is melted into liquid for injection purposes, or left in crystal form for snorting.

'cid:
a slang term for lysergic acid diethylamide, or "acid," a semisynthetic hallucinogenic drug that causes strong hallucinations.

clips:	*an abbreviated slang term for roach clips, devices for holding the butts of marijuana cigarettes smoked to the very end.*
coke:	*a slang term for cocaine.*
cool:	*the "laid back" drug-using lifestyle.*
cop a buzz:	*a slang term for getting high.*
cotton mouth:	*the dryness of the mouth that results from intoxication due to marijuana or alcohol.*
crank:	*a slang term for crystal meth, which is a soluble form of amphetamine.*
dealing:	*the sale of drugs to or between users.*
dime bag:	*a slang term for a $10 bag of marijuana.*
doobies:	*a slang term for marijuana cigarettes.*
dope:	*a slang term for marijuana or heroin.*
downers:	*a slang term for drugs that depress the central nervous system, tranquilizers, barbiturates, etc.*
druggie:	*a slang term for a regular drug user.*
free base:	*the process of refining cocaine for use in a marijuana cigarette. The result is a purified form of cocaine, and supposedly a "better high" than the street variety.*
freak:	*a slang term for one who looks and acts like a druggie.*
freak-out:	*behavior exhibited by someone on a "bad" trip.*
getting blitzed:	*a slang term for getting high.*
getting lit:	*a slang term for getting high.*
getting ripped:	*a slang term for getting high.*
getting wasted:	*a slang term for getting high.*
hash:	*hashish, a resin form of marijuana that has a higher content of the intoxicant delta-9-tetrahydrocannabinol than ordinary marijuana; it is usually smoked, but also often eaten in food or raw.*
hash oil:	*a slang term for a resinous liquid oil from the marijuana plant that also has a high content of the intoxicant delta-9-tetrahydrocannabinol.*
a head:	*a slang term for a drug user who has conformed, in appearance and lifestyle, to the user.*
herb:	*marijuana.*

hit:	*a single inhalation of marijuana, or a single dose of another drug.*
homegrown:	*a slang term for domestically grown marijuana.*
horse:	*a slang term for heroin, which is a synthesized opiate.*
huffing:	*inhaling gaseous substances to get high.*
J:	*a slang term for a marijuana cigarette, or joint.*
joint:	*a slang term for a marijuana cigarette.*
killer weed:	*a slang term for marijuana with a strong intoxicant content; some regions use the term to describe marijuana treated with angel dust or another stronger drug.*
lemmons:	*a slang term for Quaalude pills.*
lid:	*slightly more than an ounce of marijuana.*
line:	*a thin line of cocaine usually snorted off a flat glass substance, often a mirror.*
LSD:	*a slang term for lysergic acid diethylamide, a powerful semisynthetic hallucinogenic drug.*
'ludes:	*the abbreviation of Quaaludes, or methaqualone, a nonbarbiturate hypnotic-sedative drug, which is a central nervous system depressant usually found in pill form.*
MDA:	*methylenedioxyamphetamine, a psychoactive oil found in nutmeg and related to the amphetamine group, which is characterized by an intensification of feelings, talkativeness, and age regression.*
marijuana:	*the flowering tops, stems, and leaves of the female Asiatic hemp plant* cannabis sativa, *which when dried and cleaned of twigs and seeds is smoked for low-level intoxicating effects.*
mescaline:	*an alkaloid extracted from the peyote cactus, it is usually ingested in the form of a soluble crystalline powder or capsule and produces hallucinations.*
the munchies:	*a slang term for an intense hunger for sweet or salty food that occurs at a particular point in marijuana intoxication.*
mushrooms:	*psilocybin mushrooms, which have a hallucino-*

genic effect and are either brewed into a tea for drinking or eaten raw.

narc: a slang term for a police officer who investigates drug use; the term is also used for school personnel, parents, and even other teenagers who turn in people who use drugs.

nickel bag: a slang term for a $5 bag of marijuana.

opium: the natural drug extracted from poppies, which is an opiate and can be added to tobacco or marijuana and then smoked.

ounce: an ounce of marijuana or cocaine.

OZ: a slang term for an ounce of marijuana or cocaine. Also known as a Z.

papers: papers used to roll marijuana cigarettes.

party: a slang term for getting high.

PCP: phencyclidine, or angel dust, a disassociative drug used as an animal tranquilizer that produces hallucinations and comes in powder form.

pharmies: a slang term for prescribed drugs, usually in pill form, that are misused for intoxication.

pigs: a slang term for police officers.

pinwheel: a slang term for a very thin marijuana cigarette.

pipes: a slang term for a pipe specially constructed for the smoking of marijuana.

pot: a popular slang term for marijuana.

power hitter: a cylindrical device specially designed to increase the inhalation impact of smoke from a marijuana cigarette; the smoker inhales from one end and the marijuana cigarette is at the other.

Quaaludes: a methaqualone, a nonbarbiturate hypnotic-sedative drug, which is a central nervous system depressant usually found in pill form.

rainbows: a form of LSD made on paper.

reefer: a slang term for a marijuana cigarette.

resin: the thick liquid residue left in the bowl of a marijuana pipe after smoking the marijuana, which contains a high level of the intoxicant delta-9-THC.

RJS: a slang term for a type of amphetamine, or "speed," it refers to the initials written on the black capsule.

roaches: the butts of marijuana cigarettes, which contain a high concentration of resin with a high intoxicant level.

roach clips: a slang term for the devices used to hold the butts of marijuana cigarettes. They are usually tweezer-type clips or hemostats.

rush: a slang term and brand name for amyl nitrite, which comes in small, brown bottles and, when inhaled, produces an instant sixty-second high.

'script: a slang term for prescription drugs misused for getting high.

714: a slang term for a type of Quaalude that has the number 714 on it.

sheesh: a slang term for hashish, a resin form of marijuana that has a higher content of delta-9-THC than ordinary marijuana and is usually smoked.

shoot up: the use of hypodermic and needle for injection of drugs, such as Valium, speed, cocaine, angel dust, and heroin, directly into the bloodstream.

shot gun: a procedure by which one puts the lit end of a marijuana cigarette in one's mouth and blows while another stands a few inches away and inhales. This procedure increases the amount of smoke inhaled in the lungs.

'shrooms: psilocybin mushrooms, which have a hallucinogenic effect and are either brewed into a tea for drinking or eaten raw.

smack: a slang term for heroin.

smoke: a slang term for marijuana or the act of smoking marijuana.

snow: a slang term for cocaine.

speed: a slang term for amphetamines, a central nervous system stimulant that produces an aroused, excited state.

speeders: a slang term for amphetamines, central nervous system stimulants that produce an aroused, excited state.

spent: a slang term for marijuana that has been smoked until there is nothing but ashes left.

spoon: a device used for melting down drug substances for injection; it comes from the popular use of a flatware spoon for this purpose.

stash: a slang term referring to a hidden quantity of any kind of drug.

stogie: a very large marijuana cigarette.

stoned: the state of being intoxicated from drugs, especially marijuana.

stoney: a slang term for a person who is a regular user of drugs, particularly marijuana.

tea: a slang term for what users think is delta-9-THC and is usually PCP.

THC: a slang term for what users think is delta-9-THC and is usually PCP.

Thai stick: a term for a marijuana cigarette in which a stick or sticks are used to bind the loose marijuana together; the term originated in Vietnam during the war. It also refers to tobacco bound together by a stick or sticks and treated with opium; it is loosely used by some teenagers as a reference to drug-treated marijuana or tobacco cigarettes.

toke: a slang term for a single inhalation from a marijuana cigarette, pipe, or bong.

toot: a slang term for cocaine.

trip: a slang term for a hallucination experience that is induced by a hallucinogenic drug.

upper: the amphetamine group of drugs, which stimulates the central nervous system.

ups: an abbreviation for the amphetamine group of drugs, which stimulates the central nervous system.

vitamin A: a slang term for LSD.

vitamin Q: a slang term for Quaaludes, or methaqualone.

weed: a slang term for marijuana.

yellow jackets: a slang term for a type of amphetamine, or "speed."

Appendix
Suggested Readings

ADOLESCENT DRUG USE

Donlan, Joan. *I Never Saw the Sun Rise: The Diary of a Recovering Chemically Dependent Teenager.* Minneapolis: CompCare Publications, 1977.

This diary of a drug-dependent teenager from involvement with drugs to the early stages of her recovery is helpful in terms of understanding what it is like for a teenager using drugs.

Marshall, Shelly. *Young, Sober, and Free.* Center City: Hazelden, 1978.

The stories of a number of young people in trouble with alcohol and drugs and their recovery.

Newton, Miller. *Gone Way Down: Teenage Drug-Use Is a Disease.* Tampa, Fla.: American Studies Press, 1981.

A basic description, written for parents and other laymen, of the nature of teenage drug use as a disease of the feelings.

————. *Kids, Drugs, and Sex.* Tampa, Fla.: American Studies Press, 1983.

A booklet dealing with the interaction between developing drug-use disease and sexual behavior on the part of adolescents.

Toma, David, with Levey, Irv. *Toma Tells It Straight: With Love.* Harrison: Jan Publishing, 1981.

A very popular book on the whole issue of teenagers and the drug epidemic based on Toma's presentations in high schools across the country. Good, solid information in a blunt, direct form.

DRUG INFORMATION

For Parents Only: What You Need to Know About Marijuana. Rockville, Md.: National Institute on Drug Abuse, 1980.

A basic booklet for parents with good information about marijuana and its dangers.

Hafen, Brent Q., and Frandsen, Kathryn J. *Drug and Alcohol Emergencies.* Center City: Hazelden, 1980.

Good information about most of the drugs the kids use and how to react in a first-aid manner in emergencies.

Janeczek, Curtis L. *Marijuana: Time for a Closer Look.* Columbus, Ohio: Healthstar, 1980.

An illustrated book designed for teenagers with good information on marijuana.

Jones, Hardin and Helen. *Sensual Drugs.* Cambridge, England: Cambridge University Press, 1977.

A solid book based on a college course outlining all of the mood-altering drugs, their effects, and their dangers.

Malcolm, Andrew I. *The Craving for the High.* Ontario: Pocketbooks, 1973.

———. *The Pursuit of Intoxication.* New York: Pocketbooks, 1971.

These two books are readable treatments of the whole history of intoxicant use including dealing with current drugs and the dangers to modern society. Challenging and scholarly information about the whole drug scene by an eminent psychiatrist.

Mann, Peggy. *Pot Safari.* New York: Woodmere Press, P.O. Box 1590, Cathedral Station, New York, NY 10025; 1982.

This is a compilation of Peggy's popular treatment of the dangers of marijuana, which has appeared in a variety of magazines. Good information in an easily readable form.

———. *Twelve Is Too Old.* Garden City, N.Y.: Doubleday, 1980.

This is a novel for preteens dealing with the issue of one's first choices to do drugs and the dangers involved.

Nahas, Gabriel G. *Keep Off the Grass.* Oxford: Pergamon Press, 1979.

This is a more scholarly treatment of the history of attitudes toward marijuana in the United States, including the development of solid research indicating its danger.

Russell, George K. *Marijuana Today: A Compilation of Medical Findings.* New York: The Myrin Institute, 1978.

This is a brief summary of the research and findings on the dangers of marijuana.

ALCOHOL AND ALCOHOLISM

Johnson Institute. *Chemical Dependency and Recovery: A Family Affair.* Minneapolis: Johnson Institute, 1979.

This is a brief but comprehensive introduction to the nature of alcoholism as a disease with information about family involvement and recovery.

Johnson, Vernon E. *I'll Quit Tomorrow.* rev. ed., New York: Harper & Row, 1980.

This is the basic book on the nature of alcoholism and its treatment by one of the pioneers in the field.

Mann, Marty. *Marty Mann's New Primer on Alcoholism.* New York: Holt, Rinehart & Winston, 1958.

The founder of the National Council on Alcoholism gives a lot of solid information on the nature of alcoholism.

PARENT AND FAMILY RESOURCES

Brandt, Frans, and M. J. *A Rational Self-Counseling Primer.* Charlottesville: Rational Self-Counseling Institute, 1979.

A simple booklet on the use of Rational Self-Counseling techniques.

Dinkmeyer, Don and McKay, Gary D. *The Parents Handbook: S.T.E.P.* Circle Pines, Minn.: American Guidance Service, 1982.

———. *Raising a Responsible Child.* New York: Simon and Schuster, 1973.

Two excellent handbooks on parenting techniques.

Ellis, Albert and Harper, Robert A. *A New Guide to Rational Living.* Englewood Cliffs, N.J.: Prentice-Hall, 1975.

A solid book by the founder of Rational Counseling dealing with rational and irrational ways to think about life's issues.

Glenn, H. Stephen. *Developing Capable Young People.* Humansphere, P.O. Box 1566, Hurst, TX 76053.

———. *Strengthening the Family.* Potomac Press, 7100 Wisconsin Ave., Bethesda, Md. 20014.

Two booklets offering good techniques for family and child development toward caring and responsible living.

LaFountain, William L. *Setting Limits: Parents, Kids, and Drugs.* Center City: Hazelden, 1982.

A booklet giving practical guidelines to parents whose kids are starting to become harmfully involved with drugs and alcohol.

Mannatt, Marsha. *Parents, Peers, and Pot.* Rockville, Md.: National Institute on Drug Abuse, 1979.

A book by a parent who developed a self-help approach for parents to deal with kids in trouble with drugs.

Maultsby, Maxie C., Jr. *Help Yourself to Happiness: Through Rational Self-Counseling.* New York: Institute for Rational Living, 1977.

Dr. Maultsby's introduction to the use of Rational Self-Counseling techniques as a self-help way to better living.

————, and Hendricks, Allie. *You and Your Emotions.* Lexington: Rational Self-Help Books, 1977.

This is a very simple introduction to Dr. Maultsby's techniques of Rational Self-Counseling.

Miller, Sherod; Nunnally, Elam W.; and Wachman, Daniel B. *Alive and Aware.* Minneapolis: Interpersonal Communication Programs, 1975.

A popular guide to better communication between couples. The same techniques are applicable to the whole family in terms of effective communication.

Nutt, Grady. *Family Time.* Million Dollar Round Table, 2340 River Road, Des Plaines, IL 60018; 1977.

A popular guide to family building through family activities.

Powell, John. *Fully Human, Fully Alive.* Niles: Argus Communications, 1976.

A popular book on self-help techniques by a very popular author.

————. *Why Am I Afraid to Tell You Who I Am.* Niles: Argus Communications, 1969.

A popular book on communication and intimacy with self-help techniques.

Satir, Virginia. *Making Contact.* Millbrae: Celestial Arts, 1976.

A brief, easy-to-read book on communication and relationships.

————. *Peoplemaking.* Palo Alto, Calif.: Science and Behavior Books, 1972.

A somewhat technical book on families and development of healthy families by one of the leading family therapists in America.

Simon, Sidney B. *Caring, Feeling, Touching.* Niles: Argus Communications, 1976.

A good book, easy to read, on touching in human relationships; with exercises.

————. *Vulture: A Modern Allegory on the Act of Putting Oneself Down.* Niles: Argus Communications, 1977.

A fun little book with good illustrations on the whole business of self-esteem.

York, Phyllis and David. *Toughlove: A Self-Help Manual for Parents Troubled by Teenage Behavior.* Sellersville: Community Service Foundation, 1980.

A manual for parents' self-help groups whose kids are already in trouble, assisting parents to draw bottom lines for behavior.

INDEX